UNDERSTANDING
OPTIONS
TRADING
in AUSTRALIA

UNDERSTANDING
OPTIONS
TRADING
in AUSTRALIA

Christopher Tate

Wrightbooks

Also by CHRISTOPHER TATE

The Art of Trading 2nd Edition
Understanding Futures Trading in Australia
Taming the Bear

Published by and available from Wrightbooks

First published by Wrightbooks in 1997.
Updated and reprinted in May 1999. Reprinted August 2000 and July 2001.

Wrightbooks Pty Ltd
PO Box 270
Elsternwick
Victoria   3185

Ph: (03) 9532 7082
Fax: (03) 9532 7084
Email: info@wrightbooks.com.au
Website: www.wrightbooks.com.au

National Library of Australia Cataloguing-in-publication data:
    Tate, Christopher.
    Understanding Options Trading in Australia.
    2nd ed.
    Includes index.
    ISBN: 1 875857 48 6.
    1. Stock options - Australia. I. Title.
    332.63228

Cover design by Rob Cowpe
Printed in Australia by Griffin Press
ISBN: 1 875857 48 6

NOTE

The material in this book is of the nature of general comment only, and neither purports nor intends to be advice. Readers should not act on the basis of any matter in this book without considering (and, if appropriate, taking) professional advice with due regard to their own particular circumstances. The decision to trade and the method of trading is for the reader alone. The author and publisher expressly disclaim all and any liability to any person, whether a purchaser of this publication or not, in respect of anything and of the consequences of anything done or omitted to be done by any such person in reliance, whether whole or partial, upon the whole or any part of the contents of this publication.

CONTENTS

Contents (Cont'd)

INTRODUCTION

Why do some market participants trade options?

The answer to this is quite easy: the Australian exchange traded options market is one of the most dynamic, innovative and exciting of markets available and options themselves are one of the most profitable tools available to traders. Options are used by both large and small traders because of their leverage, risk management capability and capacity to greatly enhance the return on assets.

If this is so, why then don't more traders make use of this particular market?

The answer to this is also surprisingly simple: it is because of a lack of understanding among financial advisers. Traders often have their burgeoning interest in options quashed by financial advisers who have no idea about the options market. To hide this lack of knowledge, they relegate the options market almost to the realms of mysticism. It is often described as a field best left to highly sophisticated traders such as institutions.

I hope this book will redress some of these problems; treat it simply as you would a recipe book. I'll show you the basic ingredients, what happens when you mix them together and provide a few recipes. The rest is really up to your imagination.

THE BASICS

An option is merely the right but not the obligation to buy or sell a given security at a certain price within a given time. Hence, a "call" option is the *right* but not the *obligation* to buy an underlying security. Conversely, a "put" option is the *right* but not the *obligation* to sell an underlying security. A trader who buys an option as an opening transaction is referred to as the "taker" or more commonly, the "buyer". Option buyers are said to be "long" that particular option. The maximum potential loss for an option buyer is limited to the amount they paid for their option.

A trader who sells an option as an opening transaction is said to be an option "writer". The option writer receives a premium from the option buyer and is said to be "short" that particular option. In some instances, option writers can face theoretically unlimited losses.

It is important that traders understand the distinction between being an option buyer/taker and an option seller/writer. Option buyers have the right but not the obligation to exercise their option; for this they pay a premium. Option writers/sellers are under a potential obligation to either deliver stock if they are a call option writer or buy stock if they are a put option writer. For this obligation they receive a premium from the option buyer.

DESCRIBING AUSTRALIAN OPTIONS

There are only four basic components from which option descriptions are assembled:

1. *The type of option* — whether it is a call or a put

2. *The name of the underlying stock* — e.g. BHP, WMC

3. *The expiry date* — e.g. July/October, etc.

4. *The strike price of the option.*

Therefore, each option description has all four components which are assembled as follows: **BHP 2000 July call** describes a BHP call option with a strike price of $20.00 that expires in July.

STANDARDISATION OF OPTIONS

Option contracts have been standardised into four basic components comprising date of expiry, strike price, number of shares and premium. We will look at each in turn.

DATE OF EXPIRY

This is self-evident; the expiry date of an option is fixed according to one of the following cycles:

(a) January/April/July/October
(ANZ, BHP, CBA, CCA, FBG, FXJ, GMF, MIM, NAB, NBH, NCM, NMH, OSH, QRL, SGB, TAH, WBC, WPL)

(b) February/May/August/November
(ACA, AMC, ANI, BOR, BRY, CML, FLC, LLC, LHG, MAY, NCP, NCM, NDY, PAS, PDP, PLP, PLW, QAN, RER, STO, TNT)

(c) March/June/September/December
(BIL, BTR, CSR, PBL, PNI, QNI, RIO, SRP, WBC, WMC, WOW, WPL)

The Options Clearing House (OCH) stipulates that trading in options ceases at the close of trading on the Thursday preceding the last working Friday of the maturity month. If the Thursday falls on a public holiday, trading will cease on the last business day preceding the last Friday of the expiry month.

In laymen terms, this means that trading will finish in a particular option series on the last Thursday of each month. The OCH produces a calendar which defines each expiry date. This Calendar is shown in Fig. 1.1 overleaf.

Fig. 1.1 The Australian Options Market Calendar

ASX DERIVATIVES
The home of equity derivatives in Australia

Option Expiration 1997/98

JULY						
S	M	T	W	T	F	S
		1	2	3	4	5
6	7	8	9	10	11	12
13	14	15	16	17	18	19
20	21	22	23	[24]	25	26
27	28	29	30	(31)		

AUGUST						
S	M	T	W	T	F	S
31					1	2
3	4	5	6	7	8	9
10	11	12	13	14	15	16
17	18	19	20	21	22	23
24	25	26	27	[28]	(29)	30

SEPTEMBER						
S	M	T	W	T	F	S
	1	2	3	4	5	6
7	8	9	10	11	12	13
14	15	16	17	18	19	20
21	22	23	24	[25]	26	27
28	29	(30)				

OCTOBER						
S	M	T	W	T	F	S
			1	2	3	4
5	6	7	8	9	10	11
12	13	14	15	16	17	18
19	20	21	22	23	24	25
26	27	28	29	[30]	(31)	

NOVEMBER						
S	M	T	W	T	F	S
30						1
2	3	4	5	6	7	8
9	10	11	12	13	14	15
16	17	18	19	20	21	22
23	24	25	26	[27]	(28)	29

DECEMBER						
S	M	T	W	T	F	S
	1	2	3	4	5	6
7	8	9	10	11	12	13
14	15	16	17	[18]	19	20
21	22	23	24	25	26	27
28	29	30	(31)			

JANUARY						
S	M	T	W	T	F	S
				1	2	3
4	5	6	7	8	9	10
11	12	13	14	15	16	17
18	19	20	21	22	23	24
25	26	27	28	[29]	(30)	31

FEBRUARY						
S	M	T	W	T	F	S
1	2	3	4	5	6	7
8	9	10	11	12	13	14
15	16	17	18	19	20	21
22	23	24	25	[26]	(27)	28

MARCH						
S	M	T	W	T	F	S
1	2	3	4	5	6	7
8	9	10	11	12	13	14
15	16	17	18	19	20	21
22	23	24	25	[26]	27	28
29	30	(31)				

APRIL						
S	M	T	W	T	F	S
			1	2	3	4
5	6	7	8	9	10	11
12	13	14	15	16	17	18
19	20	21	22	[23]	24	25
26	27	28	29	(30)		

MAY						
S	M	T	W	T	F	S
31					1	2
3	4	5	6	7	8	9
10	11	12	13	14	15	16
17	18	19	20	21	22	23
24	25	26	27	[28]	(29)	30

JUNE						
S	M	T	W	T	F	S
	1	2	3	4	5	6
7	8	9	10	11	12	13
14	15	16	17	18	19	20
21	22	23	24	[25]	26	27
28	29	(30)				

☐ ETO & LEPO Expiration ○ Index & Ratio Expiration (NB: Ratios only expire on the Mar, Jun, Sep, Dec financial quarters)

STRIKE PRICE (EXERCISE PRICE)

This is the price at which an option buyer may exercise his right to buy or sell shares covered by a given option.

Each exercise price is generally fixed throughout the life of the option with exercise prices being set at the following intervals:

Stocks selling at:
     up to $1.00 at 10¢ intervals
     $1.00 to $5.00 at 25¢ intervals
     $5.00 to $10.00 at 50¢ intervals
     $10.00 and above at $1.00 intervals

Whilst these are generally fixed for the life of the option, they may be altered if the company whose shares are covered by the options makes a cash issue. It is important to highlight the difference between the effects of cash issues and those of a bonus. As will be highlighted in the next section, a bonus issue results in both a change in strike price and the number of shares covered by the option. A cash issue does not alter the number of shares covered by an option contract since these shares do not accrue to the option contract unless the option is exercised on a cum-issue basis.

To illustrate how adjustments are made, let's consider the following case of a trader who has taken a position in AMCOR which, during the life of the option, declares a rights issue on the basis of one new share for every five fully paid shares at a premium of 75¢. Since AMCOR is trading at $4.75, there are listed options with exercise prices of 400, 425, 450, 475 and 500. To make an adjustment to the exercise price the theoretical value of the rights is deducted from the exercise price of each contract.

EXAMPLE	
5 shares x cum-issue price $4.75	$23.75
plus cost of one new share at 75¢	0.75
	24.50
Pre-issue price	4.75
$24.50/6 new shares ex-issue price	-4.08
Rights adjustment price	0.67

Therefore, 67¢ will be deducted from the exercise price of each option contract, 400 becomes 333, 425 becomes 358 and so on.

NUMBER OF SHARES

Option contracts generally give the trader leverage over 1000 shares of the underlying stock. However, this may change during the life of the option if the underlying stock is involved in a bonus issue. If for example a company declares a 1:1 bonus then there will be an additional 1000 shares created with an exercise price half that of the original exercise price.

To illustrate this, consider the following situation. A trader has taken a position in BTR plc by buying one call contract with a strike price of $5.00. During the life of the option, BTR plc declares a 1:1 bonus. After the issue of the bonus, the trader will hold two contracts each comprising 1000 shares at a strike price of $2.50.

Irrespective of the conditions of the bonus issue adjustments are made both to the exercise price and the contract size to reflect accurately the ex-bonus market.

PREMIUM

The quoted price of an option is more often known as the premium. Option prices are quoted on a per share basis, thus to obtain the full contract price a trader has to multiply the quoted price by 1000. Hence, if BHP 2000 July calls were trading at 10¢, the price of one contract would be 10¢ x 1000 = $100.00.

An option premium splits naturally into two parts: intrinsic value and time value. Intrinsic value may be defined as the difference between the market value of an underlying security and the exercise price of a given option. For example, if BHP 2000 July calls are trading at 75¢ and BHP is trading at $20.25, then the option is said to have an intrinsic value of 25¢, this being the difference between the option strike price and the price of the underlying stock. The remaining 50¢ is time value. If our option price had remained the same whilst BHP was trading at $20.50 then our intrinsic value would have been 50¢ and our time value would be 25¢.

This relationship between time value and exercise price is shown in Fig. 1.2 opposite.

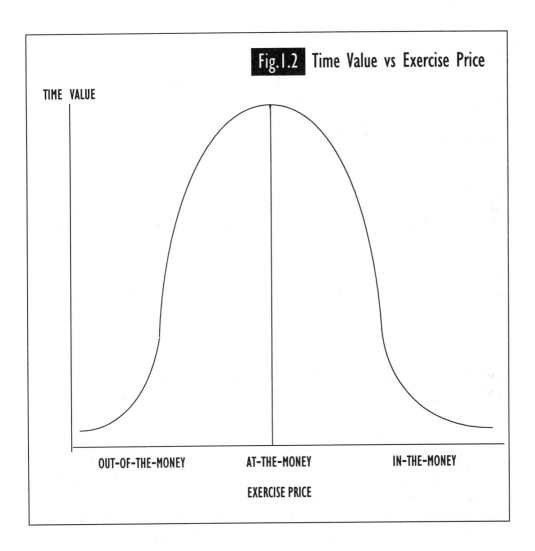

Fig.1.2 Time Value vs Exercise Price

TIME VALUE

OUT-OF-THE-MONEY   AT-THE-MONEY   IN-THE-MONEY

EXERCISE PRICE

A further refinement to our description can be added by the introduction of the terms "in-the-money" and "out-of-the-money". A call option is said to be in-the-money if the stock price is above the strike price of the option and it is out-of-the-money if the stock price is below the option strike price. If a call option is out-of-the-money, it naturally has no intrinsic value and its premium merely represents its time value.

Put options work in reverse. A put option is said to be in-the-money if the stock price is below the option strike price and out-of-the-money if the stock price is above exercise price. This is shown in Table 1.1 for put and call options having an exercise price of $20.00.

Table 1.1 In-the-Money & Out-of-the-Money

STOCK PRICE	PUT	CALL	
1,900	In-the-money	Out-of-the-money	
1,950	In-the-money	Out-of-the-money	
2000	At-the-money	At-the-money	Strike Price
2050	Out-of-the-money	In-the-money	
2100	Out-of-the-money	In-the-money	
2150	Out-of-the-money	In-the-money	

Both put and call options have their greatest amount of time value when the stock price is equal to the exercise price. As an option becomes either deeply in-the-money or out-of-the-money, its time value will shrink rapidly. This tends to be more evident in put options which decrease in time value at a greater rate once they go in-the-money compared to an equivalent call option. As we will see later, this feature is of some importance.

FACTORS INFLUENCING THE PRICE OF AN OPTION

In determining the theoretical price of an option, three major factors come into consideration. These are firstly the price of the underlying stock, the time left till maturity of the option and finally the volatility of the stock.

The overwhelming consideration in determining the price of an option is naturally the price of the underlying stock. If the stock is either well above or well below the exercise price then the remaining factors will exert little influence. This is particularly true on the day an option expires since it is worth only its intrinsic value with the other determinants being of no consequence.

The time left to maturity often exerts little influence relative to the stock price. However, there are several points which traders should be aware of. Most importantly, options are "wasting" assets. Their value declines as they age. This is shown graphically in Fig. 1.3.

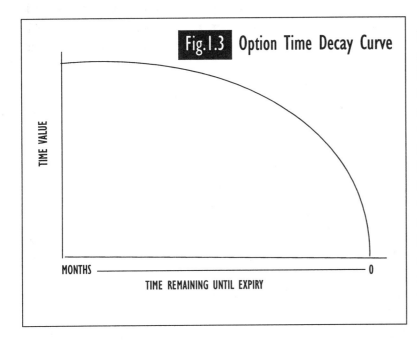

Fig.1.3 Option Time Decay Curve

TIME VALUE

MONTHS ————————————————————— 0
TIME REMAINING UNTIL EXPIRY

Note the curve is not linear, the decay in an options time value accelerates as it approaches maturity where an options price is represented only by its intrinsic value.

The consequence of this is that the longer an option has until maturity the greater time value it will command. Thus a BHP April 2000 call will be cheaper than a BHP July 2000 call which will in turn be cheaper than a BHP October 2000 call.

The volatility of the price of underlying stock also plays a part in determining an options price. It is generally accepted that the more volatile a stock the higher the price its options will command. This relationship should be regarded as self-evident since if a stock has the inherent capacity to move upward by large distances, then the buyers of calls are willing to pay higher prices and by extension sellers will demand greater compensation.

In addition to the interplay of these major influences, traders should also be aware of the effect dividends and the current risk-free interest rate may have. In the case of dividends if the underlying stock does not pay a dividend, then the option price is merely influenced by the underlying stock price, the volatility of the stock and the time left to maturity. Dividends paid during the life of a call option lower the premium. This is because the payment of a dividend naturally discounts the price of the stock. Since the market is very efficient, not only is the stock discounted, but also the call options pertaining to that stock.

The influence of the current risk-free interest rate, (i.e. 10-year bond rate) is a matter of conjecture. It is thought that the higher the rate the higher are option premiums, while the lower the rate the lower are available premiums.

Whilst traders must be aware of these determinants, ultimately it is supply and demand which dictates the actual price at which options are bought or sold. Supply and demand acts as a catalyst for all the major influencing factors.

Logically, option sellers will demand whatever price the market will bear. Similarly, buyers will only pay what they believe to be a fair price. Simple supply and demand.

OPTION PRICING MODELS

This leads me to a brief discussion on option pricing models. Much of the available published information concerns the mathematical derivation of an options price. It is highly unlikely that any trader interested in options has not at some stage been bombarded by an array of complex mathematics that many experts believe to be necessary to successfully navigate the options market. This book will not deal with these models because of their complexity and what I believe to be their irrelevance to the average trader.

Each model draws upon a series of assumptions to create what it considers to be fair value for an option. This raises two inherent problems. The first is the theoretical problem: upon what grounds are your assumptions based? The second is how you relate your theoretically-derived value to values present in the market-place.

Suppose, for example, that we wish to deal in BHP July 1950 calls and BHP July 2000 calls which are trading at say 55¢ and 28¢ respectively. Before dealing, we input our assumptions into one of our models which states that each option should have a value of 53¢ and 27¢ respectively. The quandary we now face is: do we deal at these prices or do we review the assumptions upon which our model is based? To stand aside and wait is pointless since our trading model has given us a signal to go.

This touches upon two very important considerations. Firstly, an option pricing model will give you a theoretical price; the market gives an actual price. Secondly, the options market is very efficient; buyers and sellers quickly determine what the market believes to be fair value.

CALL BUYING STRATEGIES

Just as complex discussions surrounding option pricing models and behaviour have deterred many traders, so too have discussions of option strategies. Having weathered the mathematics encountered in the early stages of all option texts, the trader is then confronted by such strange beasts as long and short butterflies, put and call ratio backspreads, condors, boxes and conversions.

Yet just as option pricing is, in reality, simple so too are option strategies. A trader may buy or sell a call or may buy or sell a put.

It is from these foundations that all strategies are created and a trader need only be familiar with these four strategies to be a successful participant in the options market. Any strategy he wishes to assemble is only limited by his imagination and how adventurous he is.

As with all explanations about option strategies we start with buying calls.

A trader's success in profiting from call buying depends upon picking the right stock and the right call — hence, it is a matter of selection and timing. Strictly speaking, call buying is not a strategy as such since it does not allow for error or for the trader to be neutral in his perception. This brings us to an important consideration: call buying is a very bullish strategy. If you are a call buyer you must be convinced that there will be a sharp upward movement in the price of the underlying stock. If the stock goes sideways or down, you will lose your money.

Having said this, why then do traders buy calls? (In Australia in 1995-96, some 10.25 million calls were traded.) There are, three primary reasons why traders buy calls. We will look at these below.

LEVERAGE

For a small outlay in cash, traders can participate in the upward movements in the price of a given stock which may result in considerable profit. To illustrate this, consider the following comparison between a call buyer and a stock owner:

BHP is selling for $18.50   BHP July 1850 call is selling for 60¢

Two months later:

BHP is selling for $19.50   BHP July 1850 call is selling for $1.00

The leverage available in the above situation can be shown as follows.

	OPTION	STOCK
Initial Cash Outlay	600	18500
Sale Proceeds	1000	19500
Profit	400	1000
% Return	66%	5.4%

This leverage that options provide enables traders to gain exposure to numerous sectors of the market for a relatively small outlay. Since all industry groups are represented by option-traded stocks a trader can, within limits, effectively assemble a portfolio of stocks representing a large proportion of the Australian stock market.

SPECULATION

This advantage applies equally to both stock-owners and those who may only be pure speculators. Suppose that you are a long-term trader with a core portfolio of non-volatile stocks and you wish to participate in a more volatile market sector without the required capital outlay and possibility of subsequent loss.

As an example, assume that you hold 5000 ANZ shares on a long-term basis, but wish to take advantage of what you perceive to be the high volatility of a stock such as NCP. Then it is possible to take positions in NCP for a small capital outlay without liquidating your ANZ holding.

STOCK PURCHASE

If we refer to our original definition of a call as being the right to purchase a given stock at a defined price, then the advantage of call buying in purchasing stock becomes immediately apparent. For example, a technical analyst may want to participate in BHP if it breaks key trend lines which may indicate a strong upward break. In such an instance, BHP may be trading at $19.00 and the trader may be willing to participate in BHP if it rallies strongly through $19.50. To do so the trader purchases a BHP 1950 call. If BHP does rally strongly and the call is in-the-money, the trader may choose to exercise the call and acquire the stock. If BHP does not increase in value, the trader has not tied up a large proportion of capital and any potential loss is limited to the amount paid for the call.

A natural extension of this may be a trader who does not wish to "miss the market". Suppose a trader is rolling out of a cash investment such as a bank bill or certificate of deposit and knows that at a certain date in the future he will have cash available. Yet in the interim he wishes to participate in a given stock because he feels a rise is imminent. This particular dilemma can be solved by purchasing an appropriate call. If a rise does occur then the call can be exercised and the stock paid for when cash is eventually available.

LIFE CYCLE OF A CALL OPTION

Perhaps the single most important concept that traders should come to terms with in this chapter is that both call and put options are wasting assets. As stated in

Chapter One, options are investments with a limited life and their value decreases naturally as they age. It can be considered a general rule that, as options approach expiry, it requires a greater movement in the underlying stock for there to be a corresponding movement in a given option.

Time is an enemy of the call option buyer. The only ally a call option buyer has is a strongly rallying stock — it is therefore necessary for a trader to choose both the stock and call option carefully.

HOW TO SELECT A CALL

STOCK SELECTION

In terms of the Australian Options Market (AOM), a trader's choice of stock is largely made for him due to the limited nature of the market. As we saw in Chapter One, there are at the time of writing only 51 available option stocks, of which only a few may offer a trader the chance to participate adequately. Despite the presence of market makers, who are compelled to deal in stocks in order to overcome illiquidity, many stocks in reality are notoriously illiquid and traders may find them hard to deal in.

The most popular traded stocks tend to be the major resource stocks such as BHP, RIO, MIM and Western Mining (WMC), industrial stocks CSR and Fosters Brewing (FBG), the three major trading banks, ANZ, NAB and Westpac (WBC), and the media giant Newscorp (NCP). The level of activity in a particular stock is defined in terms of open interest. This is a measure of the number of contracts that are outstanding. As a tool for defining which options to buy, it is of limited value since it is impossible to define whether activity is created by option buyers or sellers. However, it does help indicate which stocks are easy to deal in.

Such a limited range should not be regarded as a handicap since it helps focus the following selection criteria.

Many traders in choosing a stock do so for technical reasons such as the breaking of key trend lines. Chartists argue that the reason for this is that technical influences are more time-specific and provide a key to when and if a stock is likely to move. It is debated that fundamental factors take a non-specific time to affect share prices and that this influence may occur over a long period of time. It could also be argued that the market may have already priced in all available current and future technical information and that stock and option prices merely reflect this expectation.

Two additional points should be noted. Firstly, just because a stock appears to represent tremendous fundamental value and looks cheap, this is no guarantee that the stock will move. Secondly, many traders believe strangely enough that, having taken a position in a stock, the stock is somehow aware of this and will naturally go up. Unfortunately, this is not true, a stock does not have any friends. The most effective method of stock selection is to consider all available information both technical and fundamental. This sounds obvious and simple, however, traders often handicap themselves by not being fully informed. The best way to acquaint yourself with a stock and its movements is simply to watch it over time.

Table 2.1	Results At Expiry	
BHP PRICE	**1900 CALL VALUE**	**2100 CALL VALUE**
1900	0	0
1950	50	0
2000	100	0
2050	150	0
2100	200	0
2150	250	50
2200	300	100

Table 2.1 and Fig. 2.1 show the difference between results at expiry of buying a BHP 1900 call and BHP 2100 call.

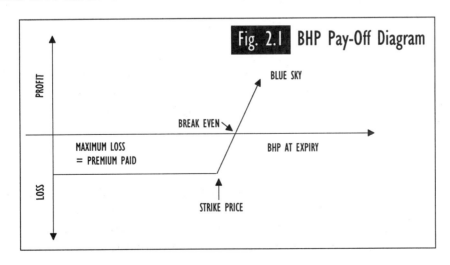

Fig. 2.1 BHP Pay-Off Diagram

WHICH CALL?

It can be considered that out-of-the-money calls offer a potential for greater reward; however, they also offer the greatest risk. Often traders will choose an out-of-the-money call because it is cheaper but this should never be a deciding factor in choosing which call to buy. For example, assume it is August and BHP is selling at $19.50, a trader surveys available calls and decides to purchase an October 2100 call because it is cheapest and he feels BHP will rally in the ensuing months. BHP rallies to $20.50 by October.

Clearly, the 2100 call will expire worthless. Consider an alternative strategy. Instead of buying the out-of-the-money call, which will experience a decrease in value even before expiry because of the influence if time decay, the trader buys a 1900 call. As the option approaches expiry, the in-the-money call will be worth at least $1.50 — comprising substantial intrinsic value and whatever time value may remain before expiry.

This brings us to a few general rules. Whereas out-of-the-money calls offer higher risk and higher reward, in-the-money calls will offer less risk and better rewards for a modest gain in the stock price. Out-of-the-money calls will offer greater reward for extreme movements in price. Thus very volatile stocks such as News Corporation which are capable of very rapid price appreciation (and depreciation) may present opportunities for call buyers who wish to buy far out-of-the-money calls.

In summary, risk-reward considerations dictate that traders largely confine their call purchases to slightly in-the-money calls. With these there is less chance of losing your entire equity, since you may recover some funds, the option you purchased will generally have some intrinsic value remaining at expiry.

Consider our initial example: if BHP had not rallied in price and was still only worth $19.50 then our 1900 call would still be worth 50¢ representing its intrinsic value.

TIMING

The certainty with which a trader feels there will be a movement in the stock will also influence the choice of which call to buy.

If you are certain that there will be a significant movement in the underlying stock in the near term, then it is logical that you strive for maximum return and not be concerned about possible losses. Thus, you would buy short-term out-of-the-money calls. However, this decision must be tempered by the knowledge that you would very rarely buy an out-of-the-money option with only a week till expiry.

If, on the other hand, you are uncertain as to the timing of any upward movement, then you would buy a longer-term call. Such a situation may arise, say, when you have been correlating the effect of a change in the value of the Australian dollar upon the price of BHP. You may be certain that a falling Australian dollar has a positive effect upon the price of BHP and that such a fall is imminent, yet you know that the timing of such falls is imprecise. Hence, you may decide to purchase a long-dated call in order to participate in the stock for as long as possible — yet retain flexibility to compensate for any margin of error. However, this extra flexibility has a cost in terms of the premium you pay. Long-dated call options have substantial time value, so even though you are compensating for the uncertainty of your timing, you are paying a higher premium to do so.

Traders must weigh up the cost of time versus any possible benefit from buying long-dated calls.

All of this should be considered in light of the fact that options are short-term investments. Traders are merely looking to make money from short-term fluctuations in price.

DELTA

The delta of an option may be defined as the amount by which a call option will increase or decrease relative to a given change in the value of the underlying security.

As a general rule, when an option is deep in-the-money its delta approximates 1. That is, any change in stock price will be reflected point for point in a change in the option price. As an easy illustration of this, consider that WMC is trading at $8.00, its 650 option, (which is deep in-the-money) is trading at say $1.60.

If WMC moves to $8.20, then the 650 option should by definition move to $1.80.

It can also generally be assumed that at-the-money options will have a delta of 0.5 and deep out-of-the-money options a delta of 0.0. Graphically, this can be illustrated as in Fig. 2.2 overleaf.

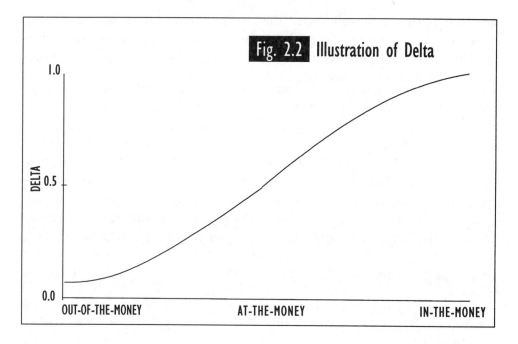

Fig. 2.2 Illustration of Delta

It should also be remembered that deltas are dynamic and change over time.

Deltas can aid call buyers in selection of their purchases because they give an indication of what percentage movement they might expect in a given call following a sharp upward movement in the price of the underlying stock. As an example, consider the following.

A trader is interested in ANZ which is currently trading at $8.00. He expects a short but limited rise in price. Should he buy the 750 or 850 call?

The following information is readily available:

Stock Price = $8.00   ANZ June 750 call price = 70¢   Delta = 0.95

ANZ June 850 call price = 25¢   Delta = 0.40

If ANZ rose by 20¢, then the 750 call should rise by 19¢ (i.e. 20 x 95¢) this represents a gain of 27 per cent. The 850 call should rise by 8¢, a gain of 32 per cent. Thus, in this simple example, the 850 call appears to be better value, provided our stock rises by the necessary amount.

STOCK VOLATILITY

Call buyers must be aware of how volatile the underlying stock is. A very simple test of volatility is to divide the change in share price range by the annual low. For example, if WMC had an annual low of $5.04 and a high of $6.90, then the volatility of the stock is defined as being:

$$\frac{\$6.90 - \$5.04}{\$5.04} \times \frac{(100)}{1} = 36.9\%$$

Therefore, in any given year, we can make the assumption that WMC can vary in price by up to 36.9 per cent. This gives us a clue as to whether our chosen stock has the historical volatility to move past our strike price. Whilst this model is not truly statistically correct, it provides us with a simple yardstick by which to be guided.

An extension of this idea is the concept of beta. Beta is defined as a measure of relative volatility, i.e. it is the price movement of a stock relative to the market as a whole. A beta of 1 dictates that a stock moves in tandem with the market; logically, a beta of 0 would imply little or no reaction to market trends.

These considerations may aid the call buyer in the following way. Assume a stock is volatile and has a high beta; the call buyer can assume that there is a good chance of movement in the stock, if there is an underlying movement in the sharemarket in general. This is of assistance if we have been noting broad-based indicators such as economic data or currencies. We know that each of these will affect the tone of the market in general and knowing a stock's beta highlights how a stock may move if the market responds to general influences.

SELECTION CRITERIA SUMMARY

So far, I have outlined a basic set of guidelines that may be used to aid the selection of which calls to buy. In summary, these can be defined as:

STOCK SELECTION —— Technical and fundamental research, aided by observation of how a stock behaves.

WHICH CALL? —— In-the-money options offer moderate reward for less risk and are best used when modest gains are expected. Out-of-the-money options are best employed where large swings in the stock price are expected. Be warned, as with all things, the greater the potential reward the greater the risk.

TIMING —— How certain are your perceptions? If totally convinced, go for maximum reward with maximum risk. If not so convinced, buy time and stay close to the money.

DELTA —— If you get it right, how far does your stock have to move before you make money and how much will you make?

VOLATILITY —— What is the likelihood of your selected stock moving at all? What does the history of the stock tell you about its ability to move?

Do not be discouraged if all this talk of timing, delta and volatility seems daunting. They are merely concepts to be familiar with and they are to a degree essential. However, with time and observation, you will develop an intuitive feel for which calls to buy.

All of this can be reduced to a single guiding rule — if you buy at-the-money or slightly in-the-money calls on stocks you are familiar with, then you will do well; provided your stock goes up. This leads me to a note of caution based upon personal observation: the majority of call buyers do not make money. No matter what selection criteria you apply, a drifting market will defeat you as easily as a falling one. Remember you are punting on a rising stock price.

DEFENSIVE ACTION

Let's suppose we have heightened our perception of the market and have applied our selection criteria. What follow up action can be taken?

Firstly, let's deal with a falling stock price. The most obvious strategy is to sell our call to cut our losses and retire. Many call buyers neglect to take even this most simple of actions — they hang on hoping for a spectacular recovery.

Experience has shown that after a sudden fall in stock price very few stocks can recover sufficiently to make the original trade profitable. Whilst there may be modest recovery, it is usually inadequate. A sudden drop in stock price is akin to falling out of a window as compared to tripping over a step. Falling out of a window is much harder to recover from, stocks are no different. A precipitous fall unsettles traders and they are understandably nervous.

Let's suppose that even given a fall in stock price and a refusal to quit the position because we believe our initial position to be correct — what can be done? Many option buyers employ a technique that is used in stock buying — they average down, that is, they buy more of the same series of calls for a lower price thereby reducing the average entry costs and hoping to profit from any recovery.

It is my opinion that it is better to quit the stock and cut your losses or employ one of the strategies that will be described later. Averaging down serves only to exacerbate what is already a losing position. Averaging down can be compared to flapping your arms in an attempt to fly rather than using a parachute.

For example, assume it's now April and you have taken a position in BHP July 2000 calls for which you paid 65¢. Your trading system indicates that BHP is on track for a subsequent lift in price — you're confident that you have made the right decision.

Suddenly, the market becomes aware of problems facing BHP. This combined with general market malaise slashes BHP's share price. Suppose you could buy enough of the same calls at a lower price to reduce your entry price to, say, 30¢.

Doesn't this mean that BHP does not have to go up as far before you show a profit? Strictly speaking. that's true.

However, even though you have lowered your entry price, BHP must still be above $20.30 at expiry for you to exit at a profit. Add to this the consideration that during the life of the call, particularly in the later stages, any movement upwards must be of such magnitude that it more than compensates for the ever-increasing effect of time-decay.

A simple general rule to follow is that the options market is dynamic and flexible; it is very good at taking your money if you are not as flexible.

LOCKING IN PROFITS

Assume, however, that our decision-making process has been correct and that we have been correct and that we have accurately predicted that our stock has moved upward in price.

What do we do now?

There are probably four general strategies we can follow. Two of them allow for cutting potential profit, whereas the other two seek to hedge our position by minimising our risk of loss, yet increase our profit potential.

Let's return to our previous example which we used to illustrate what happened if our strategy got in trouble. Let's assume BHP does rally strongly and that our BHP July 2000 call is showing a strong profit; assume it's worth $1.00.

Firstly, we could close out our position and realise our profit, thereby exiting the stock. However, if BHP continued its rally, we would have cut ourselves off from any further profit potential. We have eliminated our risk at the price of any further gain. This is the least aggressive tactic available to a trader. However, this view should be tempered by the knowledge that, if BHP falls after we close out our position, we have locked in our maximum possible profit.

Secondly, we might decide to do nothing — we simply hang on. This is the riskiest strategy available yet it appears to be the one most inexperienced option buyers adopt. In my opinion, this alternative should not even be considered. Remember if you are not flexible and dynamic you will lose your money.

Thirdly, it is possible to sell our 2000 call, recoup our initial investment and use the balance to purchase a call with a higher strike price, i.e. 2100. We are, in effect, rolling up our investment, we have recouped our initial outlay yet we are still participating in the stock — any gain on the 2100 call represents pure profit.

If BHP continues to rise, our calls will increase in value, our percentage profit will increase and yet we still have the fall-back position of being able to liquidate our 2100 calls and pocket our profit if the stock stalls.

Finally, we can put into place a slightly more advanced strategy. We continue to hold our 2000 call and against this position we write or sell the 2100 call — this creates what is known as a "bull spread". Our net position is that we are long the 2000 call and short the 2100 call. The advantage of this strategy is that we maintain our position in the stock at 2000 so we profit from the upward swing yet if the stock decays in value we are insulated to a degree by the premium we have received by selling the 2100 call.

Thus, even if both positions expire worthless, our short position will compensate for any loss on the long position. It is even possible that, depending upon the premium received for the 2100, we may not only recoup our outlay but profit from the calls expiring worthless.

Obviously, that is not the intention of the strategy. This trade will be most effective if at expiry BHP finishes between $20.00 and $21.00. In such a case the 2000 call can be sold for whatever premium is available and we pocket the premium received from the sale of the 2100 call.

The astute reader will have realised that this strategy can be used also as a defensive measure if a stock swings downward after we have taken a bullish position. It is possible to create a spread and to hedge against any downward movement yet still participate in any upward swings in the stock's movement. In this manner, a losing position is turned into a truly hedged strategy for no outlay.

CALL BUYING AND CASH INSTRUMENTS

As mentioned earlier, many traders buy call options because of the leverage they provide. For a small cash outlay, traders can take positions in a variety of stocks. This leads to an important consideration: call option buying should be *part* of an overall investment strategy. A trader should not pour all his available cash into call options merely because he can gain exposure to a wide variety of stocks. Call options enable traders to maintain a large cash position, with its inherent stability, whilst gaining exposure to the stock market.

For example, consider the case of the investor who has $100,000.00 to trade in stocks. A relatively unsophisticated approach would be to invest the total $100,000.00 in shares; this would give the trader a fairly diverse portfolio but with heightened market risk, i.e. the risk that the market may collapse. In this event

$90,000.00 in a cash instrument such as a bank bill; the remaining $10,000.00 could then be used to gain exposure to the equities market via call buying strategies.

Suppose at the end of the first year our trader has lost entirely the $10,000.00 that was exposed to the equities market, the net position is that he has still retained the $90,000.00 plus accrued interest. If we assume an interest rate of 6 per cent per annum, that would leave a cash balance of $95,400.00. Many options theorists maintain that this is the most efficient means by which to participate in the options market. Its efficiency as a strategy is undoubted; however, it is dependent upon a trader maintaining a disciplined approach as to what percentage of capital is to be exposed to the options market.

This highlights the need for traders to be disciplined in their approach. This will be a recurrent theme throughout this book. All options trading, be it simple or complex, will be inefficient without firstly an outlook as to how a stock will perform; secondly, a plan on how to take advantage of this view and finally, a defined escape route should things go wrong.

Fig. 2.3 Call Buying Summary

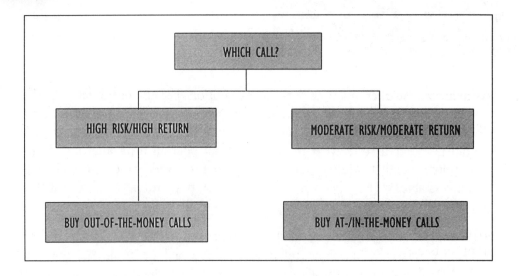

CALL WRITING STRATEGIES

If we refer back to our basic definitions in Chapter One, we will recall that call option writing is defined as the selling, or granting to a buyer of an option, the right but not the obligation to buy a given stock at a given price in the future. For this the option writer (seller) receives a premium.

It is this concept of option writing that almost always causes traders difficulty. The easiest way to remember it is as a variation of short-selling; we are merely selling something (an option) in the hope of either buying it back at a cheaper price, realising a profit, letting it expire worthless for which we also receive a profit, or being exercised and earning a capital gain.

In terms of the Australian market, call writing falls naturally into two types: scrip-covered call writing and naked call writing, which is often referred to as "cash" or "collateral" covered. Scrip-covered refers to a situation were there is underlying stock ownership and conversely going naked means there is no stock ownership involved.

SCRIP-COVERED CALL WRITING

There are two principal reasons why traders write options against stock they hold: firstly to provide downside protection and secondly, to increase the rate of return of the stock they hold. These two factors are inextricably linked; option writing for downside protection will increase the rate of return. Likewise, option writing to increase the rate of return will also offer downside protection.

As an example of this, let's assume we hold 3000 ANZ shares which were purchased for $8.70. In conjunction with this, we sell 3 ANZ July 950 calls for 30¢. By doing this we have established a scrip-covered write.

From the sale of our options, we will receive $900.00 (representing the option premium, i.e. 3 x 1000 x 30¢); if ANZ finishes below $9.50 in October the calls will expire worthless and we pocket the $900.00. Simultaneously, we have established $900.00 worth of downside protection — that is, we can have ANZ drop by 30¢ before we enter our theoretical loss zone. It must be stressed that implicit in this example is the assumption that we had purchased ANZ for $8.70 and hence we defined our theoretical loss zone as being $8.70 minus 30¢ — that is, our stock entry price minus the option premium received. In reality, traders will have to input their own entry price into the equation.

If we had purchased ANZ for $8.70 and immediately written an option against it, we would have performed what is known as a "buy and write strategy".

In performing call option-writing strategies, a trader should be mildly bullish or at least neutral in outlook.

Taking our example from above, let's examine what happens should ANZ rise in price. If ANZ rises moderately in price, we may enjoy the best of both worlds. Should ANZ finish at or just below $9.50 then our option will expire worthless and we will have the benefit of a slight rise in the price of our shares.

If ANZ rallies strongly, then we have a variety of alternatives. As with all option strategies, the alternative exists to do nothing. In such an instance, if ANZ had risen well above $9.50 and our option was then in-the-money, then our option would be exercised and our stock called away.

Our profit from such an occurrence would then comprise our initial premium of $900.00 (30¢ per share) plus the profit from the sale of our shares at $9.50. Whilst we would have made a profit on the transaction we would no longer own our shares. This brings us to a very important consideration: you must only write options against shares you are willing to sell. If you have pre-capital gains tax stock which has inherent tax advantages to it, you should NOT write options against it unless you are willing to sell it.

Instead of having our stock called away, we have a second alternative. Suppose ANZ has risen to $11.00, our 950 option will then be selling for its intrinsic value of $1.50. If we covered or bought back the option we would lose $1.20 per share or $3600.00 on our 3 contracts. However, we have removed our obligation to sell our shares at $9.50. So in reality whilst it has cost us $3600.00 to buy our option back, we have an unrealised gain of $2.30 on each share as defined by the current sale price minus original purchase price, i.e. $11.00 - $8.70 = $2.30 unrealised profit. The astute reader will have realised that by closing out our option at $9.50 we are now free to write an option at a higher strike price — thereby increasing our potential profit. Such a tactic is known as rolling up.

Notice how this profit is identical to the one we would have made if our stock had been called away. The major difference between these two alternatives is that we no longer own the stock after being exercised — whereas we retain ownership if we buy our option back. It is not always immediately apparent which of the two alternatives is best in any given situation.

However, we can define the rate of return on each possible outcome and this may aid us in making a decision:

RETURN IF NOT EXERCISED

$$\text{Return} = \frac{\text{Premium}}{\text{Initial Investment}} \times \frac{100}{1} = \frac{840}{26361} \times \frac{100}{1} = 3.18\% \text{ or } 12.7\% \text{ annually*}$$

* assuming options are written each quarter

Where:

Initial investment = 3000 ANZ @ $8.70	= $26,100	
+ 1% brokerage $261	= $26,361	
Premium = 3 contracts @ 30¢	=	$900
- brokerage of $60	=	$840

27

RETURN IF EXERCISED

Sale Proceeds (3000 ANZ at $9.50)	$28,500
Less Brokerage at 1%	(285.00)
Assume No dividends	—
Less Initial Investment	(26,361)
Plus Premium Investment	840
Premium	$2694

It should be noted that often the single most decisive factor in determining the level of profitability of a covered write is brokerage. Brokerage is paid upon exercise, although many broking firms decide on a policy of charging reduced brokerage upon exercise.

As a general rule, experience has shown that a well-structured scrip-covered write for the limited risk involved will consistently outperform any other investment. You will note that in our two examples the annualised return did not include dividends.

$$\text{Return} \quad = \frac{\text{Premium}}{\text{Initial Investmen}} \times \frac{100}{1} = \frac{2694}{26361} \times \frac{100}{1} = 10.2\% \text{ or } 40.8\% \text{ annually}$$

TYPES OF COVERED WRITES

Scrip-covered option writing falls naturally into two categories: a trader may write options that are either in-the-money or out-of-the-money. Aggressive traders who are forecasting a substantial fall in share prices would write deep in-the-money options for greater premium return. In our first example, we were fairly conservative; our option was out-of-the-money when sold.

To illustrate the difference between alternatives, let's assume that we have written 3 ANZ July 900 call options for which we have received 75¢. As noted earlier, this is a very aggressive strategy; we have predicted that at the end of the life of our option ANZ will be below $8.25 and that our option will expire worthless. If ANZ should rally strongly then we have two choices: firstly do nothing and be exercised or buy our option back.

Let's assume a range of alternatives are available and that we try to buy our options back at expiry.

From this table, several points are evident. Firstly, our maximum profit is limited to our initial credit but our loss in attempting to buy back our position is theoretically unlimited (obviously if the stock rose too far we would merely wait for exercise and not incur such a loss). Our breakeven point is equal to the strike price at which we sold our call, plus the premium received.

ANZ at Expiry	Call Value	Profit/ Loss
800	0	+75
825	0	+75
850	0	+75
875	0	+75
900	0	+75
925	25	+50
950	50	+25
975	75	+0
1000	100	-25
1025	125	-50
1050	150	-75

It should be remembered that irrespective of how far ANZ rises in price, we are obligated, if exercised, to deliver our stock at $9.00 per share. However, our true sale price is $9.00 + 75¢, being $9.75. If ANZ rises above our breakeven point, then we would have a theoretical loss because we would be selling our stock at below what is the current market value. Yet if ANZ falls sharply our call will expire worthless and we will retain our shares.

Once again, we can calculate rates of return:

RETURN IF NOT EXERCISED

$$\text{Return} = \frac{2190}{26361} \times \frac{100}{1} = 8.3\%$$

Where:

Initial Investment	= 3000 ANZ @ $8.70	= $26,100
	+ 1% brokerage $261	= $26,361
Option Premium	= 3 contracts @ 75¢	= $2,250
	- brokerage of $60	= $2,190

RETURN IF EXERCISED

It is immediately apparent that such an aggressive strategy is of limited value in a rising market — its success depends upon a sharp fall in the stock to below the

Sale Proceeds (3000 ANZ at $9.00)	$27,000
Less Brokerage at 1%	(270)
Assume No Dividends	—
Less Initial Investment	(26,361)
Plus Premium Investment	2190
Premium	2559

written strike price. If the stock finishes above the exercise price then the option will be exercised. As a general rule, you should not write/sell call options that have a lower strike price than your original entry price. The AOM is very efficient and if an arbitrage opportunity exists then, on the balance of probabilities, you will be exercised and as we have seen a pre-emptive exercise will cause a loss.

$$\text{Return} = \frac{\text{Profit}}{\text{Initial Investment}} \times \frac{100}{1} = \frac{2559}{26361} \times \frac{100}{1} = 9.7\%$$

MECHANICS OF OPTION WRITING

Having described the fundamental theory behind scrip-covered option writing, it is necessary that the trader be cognisant of the procedural requirements of option writing.

If you are writing options against stock you already own, then it is necessary to lodge your scrip with the Options Clearing House (OCH). Along with this, you lodge a bulk scrip depository receipt and standard transfer. Although it is unlikely because of carrying costs that your option will be exercised early, it is possible and you must be ready for it. Exercise and assignment happen automatically; the first you will know about it is when your broker receives an exercise notice from the OCH and from this point the events cannot be altered. It should also be stressed that exercise is totally random — it cannot be predicted nor can it be reversed.

Whilst your scrip is held by the OCH you remain at all times its owner. All benefits of stock ownership accrue to you: all dividends, bonuses or other issues remain yours.

DEFENSIVE ACTION

As we have seen in the earlier section an upward swing in the stock will only enhance our underlying profitability where the strategy has been carefully structured. If we leave our strategy untouched we will exit the stock at a profit.

However, consider another example. Suppose we hold ANZ shares purchased at $8.70 and when ANZ was trading at $9.20 we sold ANZ 950 July calls for 30¢ thereby providing an implicit 30¢ downside protection. Let's now assume that ANZ falls heavily and is trading at $8.30 — we have an unrealised loss of 40¢ on our stock. What action can we take to enhance our position?

As our stock falls so too does our option. The first step to take is to buy the option back thereby locking in our premium. Secondly, we must look for another option with a lower strike price and/or later expiry date. Such a tactic is generally referred to as "rolling down". Suppose in our example we could buy our original option back at 0¢ (i.e let it expire worthless) and sell an ANZ July 850 call at 30¢ this would provide us with an additional 30¢ downside protection. Hence our downside breakeven has been lowered from $8.40 to $8.10. So, rolling down has simultaneously given us further protection and increased our income if the stock stabilises.

The quandary that traders face is when to begin defensive action; it is quite possible for a stock to sustain a heavy fall and then suffer a reversal. Many traders use historically derived technical support levels and will begin defensive action if these levels are breached. However, we should be wary of being caught by reversals. If we have rolled down too soon a rebound may see us locked into the stock on the basis of having a deep in-the-money call which will be exercised at the lower strike price.

NAKED CALL OPTION WRITING

If a trader writes/sells a call option without owning the underlying stock, then he is said to have a written a "naked option". Naked option writing has a limited potential profit and theoretically unlimited loss.

To illustrate this relationship assume we have written WMC Sept 900 calls for 15¢. Our maximum profit potential is limited to 15¢ — the premium we have

WMC at Expiry	Call Value	Profit/ Loss
850	0	+15
875	0	+15
900	0	+15
925	25	-10
950	50	-35
975	75	-60

received. Yet our potential for loss is unlimited. If WMC rallies strongly, then we risk having to buy back our option at parity or being exercised. Remember that by writing a call option we have obligated ourselves to deliver a given number of shares at a certain price if required to do so. Given that we have written our option at the $9.00 strike price, if WMC finishes above $9.15, our breakeven, we will be in a loss situation. A range of possible outcomes is shown in the table. Our breakeven point is determined by adding the premium to our strike price.

Note how our profit is limited to our initial credit; yet once we reach our breakeven point our loss is unlimited if we were to attempt to buy our position back (see the WMC pay-off diagram for writing a call in Fig. 3.1).

A naked option writer will not necessarily lose money if the stock moves up — a loss will only be incurred if the underlying share finishes above our breakeven point. Clearly, even though our loss is theoretically unlimited, in reality this is not so since a stock cannot rise to infinity. But it is worth remembering that options values inflate very quickly on the back of speculation of further price rises.

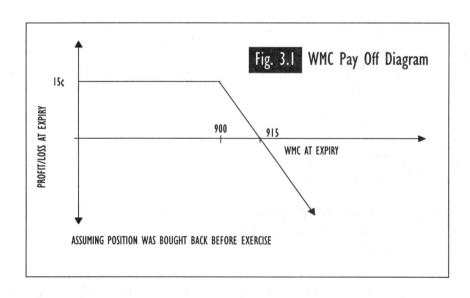

Fig. 3.1 WMC Pay Off Diagram

15¢

PROFIT/LOSS AT EXPIRY

900   915   WMC AT EXPIRY

ASSUMING POSITION WAS BOUGHT BACK BEFORE EXERCISE

DEGREE OF AGGRESSIVENESS

The risk/reward criteria for this strategy are dependent upon the aggressiveness of the trader. Very aggressive traders would consider writing an in-the-money call thereby granting themselves a larger potential profit but with accompanying higher risk. Conversely, the writer of an out-of-the-money call will achieve a smaller return but with less risk.

If a trader is very bearish and is seeking to trade the short side of a stock for a small profit, then he should consider selling deep in-the-money calls. Referring back to our early discussions, we will remember that deep in-the-money calls have a delta of 1 — that is, the option will move in parallel to the underlying stock. If the stock falls substantially, then profits can be made. However, our option with its delta of 1 will also move up with the underlying stock causing what may be substantial losses. In undertaking such a strategy, the option writer should be careful to only sell those options which will have some time value left so as to avoid exercise. It is not usual for traders to sell at-the-money calls. Normally, a trader who wants to limit the risk will write out-of-the-money calls whereas the trader who wants larger quicker profits will sell in-the-money options.

DEFENSIVE ACTION

As previously stated, if our underlying stock rises above our breakeven point, then we lose money either by having to buy our option back or by being exercised and having to deliver stock. However, this can be avoided by carefully designed fall-back action. Firstly, the breakeven point needs to be carefully defined. Once this point is reached, we have to decide whether to quit the stock permanently.

It is essential that losses be culled immediately. To not do so is to invite disaster. It should be noted that if you have written a naked call then you are on the wrong side of the trend. Such a situation should not be allowed to persist.

UNDERSTANDING MARGIN REQUIREMENTS

It is important for traders in the options market to understand that their obligations when trading options are often markedly different from when trading shares. The most apparent of these differences becomes obvious when options are written. Throughout this book reference has been made to strategies where options are written or short sold. Undertaking any of these strategies brings with it certain obligations. Because of the confusion that often surrounds these situations it is necessary to review your obligations before moving on to a discussion of how the margining system operates.

The writer or seller of a call undertakes to sell to the call taker or buyer the underlying share at a fixed price on or before the expiry date. In this situation if the call buyer decides to call away the stock from you, you have to supply that stock at the price specified in the options contract. For example, if you have sold a BHP July 2000 call and that call is exercised by the buyer you have to supply BHP at $20.00, irrespective of the current market price. Such a situation presents you with no downside risk if you own the underlying share. The only risk you face is the opportunity cost of having your BHP called away in what may be a rising market.

If you are, however, a naked option writer then you are faced with a very serious dilemma. Using the same example consider that you have written a BHP July 2000 call but you have done so without owning any BHP shares. Consider that BHP has risen to $23.00 and the call you have written is exercised then you have to sell to the call buyer BHP at $20.00, despite the fact that BHP is trading in the market for $23.00. So you have to buy BHP at $23.00 and sell it for $20.00, a loss of $3.00 (plus brokerage but less the option premium received). If you had sold ten contracts then you would be looking at a loss of around $30,000.00. Once you have received your exercise notice there is nothing you can do about it, default is not an option.

A set of analogous responsibilities applies to the sellers or writers of put options. In writing a put you have obligated yourself to take delivery of the underlying share at the price specified by the option strike price. For example, if you had sold a BHP 2000 July put, then you have guaranteed that you will, if required, take delivery of BHP at $20.00 per share irrespective of the market price. If you assume that BHP has fallen to $17.00 and your contract is exercised then you are required to take delivery of BHP at $20.00. If you are not in a financial position to hold BHP then you will have to on-sell BHP to the market. In doing so, you are crystallising a loss of approximately $3.00 per share. If you were naked 10 contracts then you would be looking at a loss of $30,000.00 if you were not in a position to hold indefinitely $200,000.00 worth of BHP.

Many new entrants to the options market are often confused and irritated by the need for margins when writing options. If you have been one of those who is irritated by margins, consider either of the above examples and whether you could survive the financial strain imposed upon you by such a situation. Margins operate for many reasons. They protect the financial viability of the options market by guaranteeing that any obligations you might have are met. They protect your broker from your possible default in a situation where the financial burden of a trade becomes too great. Finally, and most importantly, they protect you by giving an exact idea of the status of your trade. Nothing focuses the mind like repeated margin calls. Consider how the system would work if, instead of progressive margining, you were faced by the need to make a single lump sum payment at the termination of a position. Such a system would be prone to default as traders unaware of their obligations throughout the life of the trade collapsed under the weight of a single payment.

HOW TO CALCULATE MARGINS

At first glance the margining system the OCH uses which goes by the name Theoretical Intermarket Margining System (TIMS) appears rather complicated. However, like everything to do with options it becomes much simpler when it is broken down into its component parts.

SCRIP-COVERED OPTIONS

In the situation of a buy and write which was described earlier in this book, an options trader sold options against stock they already owned. For example, if you owned 5000 WMC shares and sold 5 WMC calls against this stock position you would have established a scrip-covered write. The shares you own are lodged with the OCH and they serve as collateral for this strategy. As such you incur no further margin obligations. If you are exercised you simply fulfil your obligation by selling the underlying shares.

There is a second method whereby someone who owns shares may use those shares as collateral for the purposes of writing options. The OCH will assign a collateral value to shares that have been lodged as security, this system works in the following manner.

The OCH has established three tiers of shares acceptable to be lodged as security:

> ➤ **Tier One** in the jargon of the OCH refers to *securities approved as underlying securities under Rule 7.4.1 and securities which the criteria*

for approval under that Rule but which are not currently approved. In simple terms any share that has exchange traded options may be lodged as collateral. For example, you could lodge ANZ shares for the purposes of writing RIO options.

➢ **Tier Two** is any share or units in entities within the ASX Fifty Leaders which do not fall within the shares listed in Tier One.

➢ **Tier Three** is any exchange traded security of Tier One shares, other than fully paid ordinary shares that meet the following criteria: issued capital represented by the securities must be a minimum of $100 million, the minimum monthly volume must be in excess of 100,000 units and the minimum closing price must be at least 50¢.

In defining how much the collateral you have lodged is worth, the OCH applies a discount to the market value of your shares. The purpose of applying a discount is to guard against a sudden change in the market value of your shares. Such a treatment provides both you and the OCH with a buffer against unexpected market volatility. At present this discount is 30 per cent of the total market value of the shares you have lodged.

For example, if we assume you have lodged 5000 BHP with a market value of $18.00, the market value of your basket of shares is $90,000.00. In applying a collateral value to these shares the OCH subtracts 30 per cent of the market value of the shares. As 30 per cent of $90,000.00 is $27,000.00 the value of your collateral is $63,000.00. You therefore have $63,000.00 available to fulfil your margin obligations.

Collateral must be lodged with the OCH by 4pm of the day in which the trade is initiated. So if you put a trade into the market in the morning you must lodge your collateral by 4pm of the same day. If you do not the OCH will treat it as an uncovered position and full margins are payable in cash by 11am of the following morning.

As well as taking shares as security the OCH will accept a range of other financial instruments such as bank guarantees, certificates of deposit and non bank bills of exchange.

CALCULATING MARGINS FOR EXCHANGE TRADED OPTIONS

The total margin payable by traders when they have written a naked position is made up of two components, the premium margin and risk margin.

> *Premium margin* represents the current price you would get for your option if it were liquidated at the end of the day.

> *Risk margin*, which is also known as the initial margin, is the amount that represents that largest likely daily move in the value of the option. The calculation of this variation is based upon historical models of the price movements and current market volatility of the underlying share.

CALCULATING PREMIUM MARGINS

Let's assume you have written a BHP Sept 1850 call for $1.13 then the premium margin would simply be the premium you received, $1,130.00. Remember the terms price and premium are interchangeable, so if you are having difficulty working out your premium risk just think of it as being a deposit that is equivalent to the price of your option. The situation is similar for the buyers of options but in this case the premium you have paid is treated as a credit, not a debit as in the case of written options. You might ask what relevance is an example of the situation with bought options. However, bought options play a role in determining margins.

If, for example, you use our original example of having sold a BHP Sept 1850 call for $1.13 you would be liable for a margin of $1,130.00. However, if in conjunction with the short in BHP you had also bought an RIO Sept 2232 call for 90¢ or $900.00 then you would be eligible for what is termed an "offset".

The practice of offsets allows portfolios of options to be matched against one another. Such a practice recognises the reality that a market cannot simultaneously go both up and down, therefore as one position loses value another gains value.

The offset in our example works in the following way:

> Short 1 BHP Sept 1850 call @ $1.13 = $1,113.00 debit margin
> Long 1 RIO Sept 2232 call @ $0.90 = $ 900.00 credit margin

The total margin position is calculated by subtracting the credit margin from the debit margin. In this example there is a total premium margin payable of $213.00. The OCH, in calculating the total premium margin, seeks to take into consideration the net margin position of all open positions across all option classes for that account. To calculate your premium margin is simply a matter of summing all your premiums.

We can further illustrate this by extending our example and adding two more positions:

Short BHP Sept 1850 call @ $1.13 = $1,130.00 debit margin

Long RIO Sept 2232 call @ $0.90 = $900.00 credit margin

Short NAB Oct 1850 put @ $0.73 = $730.00 debit margin

Long WMC Dec 750 put @ $0.17 = $170.00 credit margin

A bit of simple arithmetic gives us our total premium margin position, i.e. $1,130.00 - $900.00 + $730.00 - $170.00 = $790.00 debit margin. Note that this is a debit because the dollar value of our short trades exceeds that of our long trades. There is also no difference in the treatment of short puts and calls versus long puts and calls, any short or written position can offset any long or bought position.

CALCULATING RISK MARGINS

Risk margin is defined by the OCH *as being the largest probable daily move in the value of an option based upon a study of the historical movement in price and the current market volatilities of the underlying security.* In other words the OCH looks at how volatile a share has been for a period of six months, this gives a guide to the possible range of movement that a share may move in during a period of normal market activity. This study of a share's volatility generates a figure known as the "margin interval" which is expressed as a percentage.

If a share such as WBC has a current market value of $7.30 and its margin interval has been calculated to be 8 per cent — which is equivalent to 58¢ either side of the current market price — then based upon the margin interval the stock is unlikely to either fall below $6.72 or rise above $7.88 the next trading day. In essence we have established a theoretical range based upon a review of historical data within which our stock may move.

However, such information on its own is largely useless in defining our margin commitments. In order to determine how this may affect our margin commitment it is necessary to understand how a move in the underlying share will affect our option. To do this it is necessary to review the concept of delta. As defined earlier in this book, the delta is the amount an option will move given a specific rise in the underlying stock. If an option had a delta of 1 then for every 1¢ move in the underlying share the option would also move 1¢. Conversely if an option had a delta of 0.5 then the underlying share would have to move 2¢ for the option to move 1¢.

To take our WBC example our margin interval is 8 per cent or 58¢ based upon the current market value of $7.30. Let's assume that we have sold the WBC Oct 775 call for 30¢ and that this option has a delta of + 0.26.

To calculate our risk margin we have to recalculate the value of our option, taking into account the range of possible prices as defined by our margin interval. So our risk margin is calculated by multiplying our maximum rise in price by the delta of our option:

$$58¢ \times 0.26 = 15¢$$

Our total margin commitment is our premium margin (current market price) plus our risk margin:

$$30¢ + 15¢ = 45¢ \text{ or } \$450.00 \text{ per contract}$$

It should be noted that we only have to revalue our option on the upside since we are only interested in the maximum possible move against our position. A fall in WBC would add value to our position. In calculating your margin requirements the OCH uses an option pricing model known as the Cox-Rubenstein Binomial Model and what is termed modern portfolio theory. Both are beyond the scope of this book. However, the above example gives you an idea of how margins work and a rough guide to their application.

When actual margins are levied against your account you are going to have to trust that the figures supplied to you by the OCH and your broker are correct. To calculate all the margins required by your account, particularly if you are trading a basket of options, is largely a waste of your time and effort and requires a mathematical competency that is beyond most traders. If you have difficulty in accepting the figures you are given all I can say is that in all my time dealing in options I have never seen an error in a margin statement. If you baulk at the level of margins required to be paid then you don't fully understand that margins are there for everyone's protection.

Clients who used to complain about margins often reminded me of the old story of the customer in the Porsche dealer who was worried about fuel economy; if you can't afford the petrol you can't afford the car. The same is true for margins, if you can't afford them then you should not be trading this particular side of the market.

Fig. 3.2 Call Writing Summary

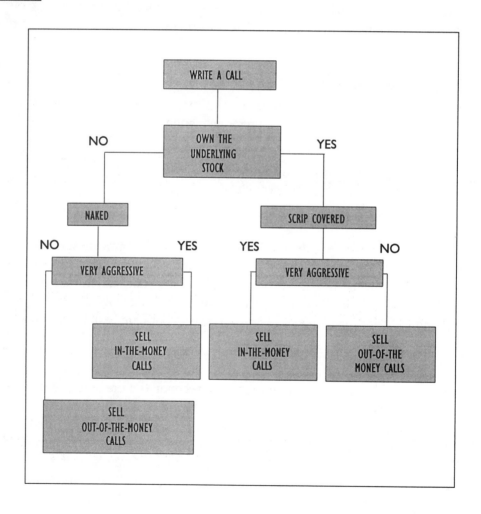

PUT BUYING STRATEGIES

Chapter Four

- ☑ How to Select a Put
- ☑ Defensive Action
- ☑ Locking in Profits

Just as call buying is a bullish strategy, put buying is a bearish strategy and can be a very effective tool in a falling market. A put option buyer is convinced there will be a downward movement in the stock during the life of the option.

In many instances the concepts outlined in Chapter Two may be reversed and applied to puts with equal efficiency.

An initial difference put buyers must come to terms with is the concept of in-the-money and out-of-the-money. In reference to call options an option which has a strike price lower than the stock's current price is said to be in-the-money. An option with a strike price which is higher than the stock price is out-of-the-money. The situation is reversed with put options. A put option is considered to be in-the-money when the strike price of the option is higher than that of the stock.

Put options do not trade in the same volume as call options, yet traders buy them for many of the same reasons that they buy call options. In practice, there are two prime reasons.

LEVERAGE

Put option buying is a leveraged alternative to short selling stock. In short selling a stock, a trader sells a stock he does not own in the hope of buying it back at a cheaper price, thereby profiting from a fall in the price. This is a very risky strategy should the stock rise sharply. Alternatively, for a small cash outlay, a trader can profit substantially from a fall in a stock price, at limited risk. A short seller's risk is theoretically unlimited.

DOWNSIDE PROTECTION

The purchase of a put can be used to limit the downside in stock that is already owned. When a trader owns stock and a put covering that same stock, then there is limited downside during the life of the put.

For example, if we purchase RIO at $17.75 and we simultaneously purchase an RIO July 1750 put at 30¢, the put gives us the right to sell our stock at $17.50. Therefore the maximum we can lose on our stock is $17.75 - $17.50 = 25¢, see Fig. 4.1. Since we have paid 30¢ for our put, our maximum potential loss during the life of our put is 55¢. However, if the stock goes up we stand a chance of losing our investment in the put, yet this is compensated for by unrealised gains on our stock.

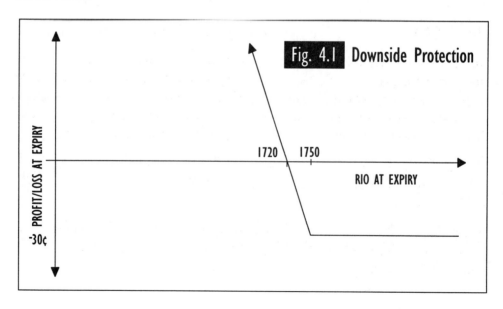

Fig. 4.1 Downside Protection

Thus, our put purchase has acted like an insurance policy with a limited life.

In general, there are two types of trader who may opt for this approach. The first is long-term trader who wants some protection during the life of the put. As a long-term holder, it is unlikely that such a trader will actually sell his stock via exercise. The purchase of a low cost put will aid in rectifying some of the damage done to a portfolio by sudden drops in price.

The second type of traders comprise those who are taking a position in a stock and may also consider the purchase of a put. This will aid in offsetting any losses if they have entered the stock at the wrong time. It is possible to simultaneously buy the stock and the put.

HOW TO SELECT A PUT

STOCK SELECTION

This has been adequately covered in Chapter Two. Although the discussion there focused on call options it applies similarly to selecting stocks for writing puts.

WHICH PUT?

Risk/reward considerations once again dictate which puts to buy. As is the situation with call options, buying an out-of-the-money put offers the trader higher potential rewards and higher risk. If a stock drops sharply, then the return on the cheaper out-of-the-money put will be substantial. However, if the stock drops only marginally then the in-the-money put will show a better return.

To illustrate this relationship consider the following situation: BHP is trading for $18.50 and we have the choice of buying either a July 1800 put at 35¢ or a July 1900 put for 50¢.

If BHP were to drop to $17.00 at expiry then the July 1800 put would be worth $1.00 — a profit of 65¢ or 186 per cent. The July 1900 put would be $2.00 — a profit of $1.50, or 300 per cent.

Therefore, in a sharp downward movement, the in-the-money put clearly has a greater potential profit. However, if BHP only declined to $18.00 by expiry then the 1800 put would expire worthless whereas the 1900 put would enable us to recoup our investment of 50¢.

This brings us to a general rule — *unless a large downward swing is anticipated concentrate on in-the-money puts.*

TIMING

The general rules on timing covered in Chapter Two also apply to puts. However, a few points are worth noting. Put options have slightly different time decay characteristics. With call options it is only possible to buy substantial time value at a higher premium. With put options, it is not unusual to see very little time value even in long-dated options.

It is not unusual to see the following situation shown in Table 4.1.

Table 4.1 Time Value in Calls and Puts

Pacific Dunlop (PDP) trading at $4.75			
Call Options	Price	Put Options	Price
May 475	17¢	May 475	12¢
Aug 475	42¢	Aug 475	22¢
Nov 475	63¢	Nov 475	28¢

Notice how there is substantially more time value in the calls versus puts. This affects the timing of our decision in the following way.

If we can purchase extra time for relatively little extra premium, then we can effectively hedge our timing at very little cost. This is in direct contrast to the situation with call options where increased time value is reflected directly in increased premium.

Consequently, when purchasing a put it may be worth considering whether to buy a long-dated put, if the time value is small, relative to the near-dated puts.

DELTA

In Chapter Two, delta was defined as the amount by which an option will move given a movement in the underlying stock. Put options also have deltas, but obviously they are negative numbers which reflect the fact that the option price and the share price are inversely related, i.e. as a stock price goes up, the put option price comes down and vice versa.

Therefore, the delta of put options will have values ranging from 0 to -1. As a general rule, the delta of an out-of-the-money put is close to zero whereas the delta of an in-the-money approximates -1.

To demonstrate the relationship between a put option price, its delta and the stock price, consider the following:

EXAMPLE

NCP is trading at $5.75 and the 550 put option, which is out-of-the-money, is selling for 15¢ and its delta is -0.28, then if NCP dropped in price to $5.60, theoretically the option should increase in price to 19.2¢. This is calculated by multiplying the fall in the share price (15¢) x option delta + initial option price (i.e. 15 x 0.28 + 15 = 19.2). It should be noted that the delta of the option would change dynamically as the stock falls in price.

STOCK VOLATILITY

The text in Chapter Two covers the discussion on stock volatility adequately for both puts and calls.

DEFENSIVE ACTION

Just as a broad range of tactics were available to the call buyer, so too are they available to put option buyers.

In Chapter Two, I dealt firstly with a falling option price and in that section I outlined the objections to the concept of averaging down. The arguments against that strategy hold true to put option buyers. I will not repeat the objections here, but suffice to say that averaging down with put options rarely works and should be avoided.

LOCKING IN PROFITS

Once again, if we are presented with a potential profit we can opt for one of four possible alternatives:

> Firstly, the position could be closed and we pocket our profit and retire. Such a strategy removes all risk, but it also removes any further profit potential. Once again, this is a non-aggressive strategy.

> Secondly, we could elect to do nothing — as stated before, this tactic shouldn't even be considered.

> Thirdly, we may, in effect, roll down our investment by selling our initial put option, recouping our original costs and investing the rest in a lower priced put. This allows us to retain our original investment — thereby reducing the risk of capital loss while allowing us to maintain a position in the stock, and possibly enhance our profit potential. In this strategy we are allowing the trend to be our friend.

> Finally, we may create a spread by selling an out-of-the-money put against our original long position. In such a situation, we can still profit from any further downward movement in the stock and if it reverses direction, our short position will decrease in value and insulate us from any severe price rise in the underlying stock. Once again, this alternative also lends itself to rectifying a losing position since the premium income from the short position would help offset any unrealised loss. Naturally, this strategy works best if the underlying stock stabilises in price.

Fig. 4.2 Put Buying Summary

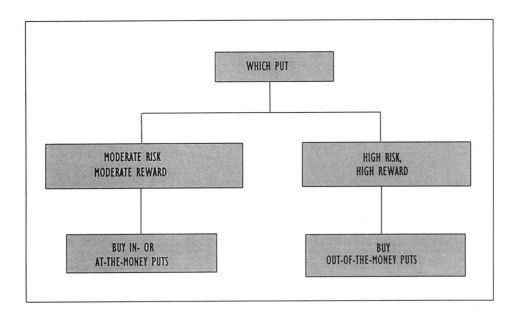

PUT OPTION WRITING

Chapter Five

☑ Naked Put Writing

☑ Defensive Action

☑ Writing Puts to Acquire Stock

In buying a put, a trader has paid a premium for the right but not the obligation to sell their stock at a given price some time in the future. Hence, the writer of a put is obligated to buy that stock at the given strike price.

The easiest way to remember this is to realise that a put option writer will have stock put to him if the strategy goes wrong.

Traders may write puts for two general reasons: the first is merely to speculate on a rising market. The second is an innovative way to buy stock at below market prices.

NAKED PUT WRITING

SPECULATION

Naked put writing is the most commonplace of put writing strategies — it is inherently bullish and theoretically has unlimited loss. Let's take a look at an example.

Table 5.1 Possible Outcomes

NCP at Expiry	Put Value	Profit/ loss
600	50	-10
625	25	+15
650	0	+40
675	0	+40
700	0	+40

EXAMPLE

Assume we are bullish on NCP and seek to take advantage of any upward swing in the stock price. NCP is currently trading at $6.00 and we decide that the stock should advance from this price. So we sell or write an NCP 650 August put for which we receive 40¢ — this 40¢ represents our maximum profit potential yet our loss can be theoretically unlimited.

The possible range of outcomes is shown in Fig. 5.1.

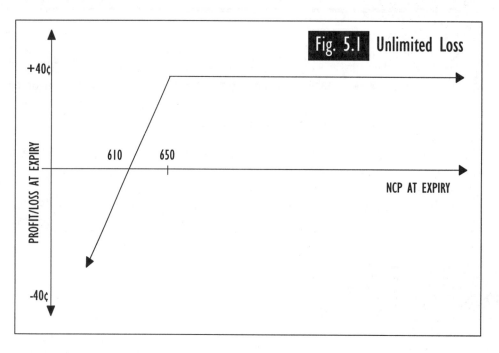

Fig. 5.1 Unlimited Loss

Note how our profit is limited to our initial premium but our loss is unlimited. In this situation, it is assumed that the option was bought back before expiry, thereby eliminating the possibility of being exercised.

It should be noted that being exercised will also result in a greater loss than buying the option back. Such an anomaly results from brokerage and stamp duty costs, and the potential inability for a trader to sell stock that has been put to them at an adequate price. Put writers will be exercised if the market falls heavily. This will result in them paying over-the-market prices for stock and then attempting to on-sell this stock into a falling market.

How aggressive a trader wishes to be will determine which put to write. The least aggressive option is to write an out-of-the-money put; that is, write a put with a strike price below the current market price of the stock. Such a strategy offers moderate reward for less risk.

A very aggressive put writer may seek to write a deeply in-the-money put for which he will receive a larger premium. However, for this greater reward, greater risk is assumed.

DEFENSIVE ACTION

As with call writing, the put option writer must have a fall-back plan if the situation goes awry.

The simplest of actions is merely to buy back the position and take the resultant loss. Often this is possible without incurring too great a loss since a put option will lose its time value very quickly once it is in-the-money. In closing out a position immediately we recognise the potential for a loss, we dramatically limit the size of the loss. In doing so we admit that we are on the wrong side of the trend — thereby freeing ourselves to take advantage of the underlying trend instead of attempting to trade against it. Hoping and hanging on are not strategies that will guarantee our long-term survival.

WRITING PUTS TO ACQUIRE STOCK

Some traders take the innovative step of writing puts against stock they wish to acquire below its current market price. This approach is appropriate for a sideways trending market that is merely drifting. Such a market offers the chance for the trader to be exercised without the market swinging too far away from the entry point.

Imagine we are a trader wishing to take a position in NAB which is currently trading at $18.50; however, we consider it to be a better buy at $18.00 or below. So we write an NAB 1850 July put for which we receive 75¢. If NAB is below $18.00 at expiry, there is a good probability that we will have the stock put to us at $18.50. If such a situation occurred, we would have bought NAB for $17.75, representing the option strike price minus the premium we have received. Therefore, if NAB is between the range of $17.75 to $18.50 at expiry, we will have effectively bought it at below market price.

If NAB is above $18.50 at expiry, we merely pocket the premium we have received and try again. The downside to such a technique is that if NAB fall substantially, say to $17.00, we would still be paying an effective $17.75 per share.

Fig. 5.2 Put Writing Summary

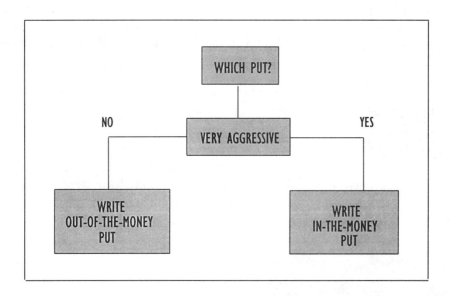

PUTS AND CALLS

So far we have examined possible strategies that involve the buying or selling of puts and calls in isolation from one another. More advanced techniques enable us to take advantage of the inherent qualities of puts and calls by using them in conjunction with one another. The two most basic of these strategies are the "combination" and the "straddle".

THE COMBINATION

As the name suggests, this strategy merely involves the buying of both a put and a call that have different terms. Option buyers may have already inadvertently created a combination without realising it. Suppose that the following situation had occurred:

EXAMPLE

A trader purchased a WMC 900 July call for 25¢, when the stock was $8.90, following which the stock rose to $9.50; the call was worth at least 50¢, representing its intrinsic value. To lock in this profit and protect against any downside, the trader bought a WMC July 1000 put for say 12¢. After the purchase of the put, the trader's net position was that he was long the WMC 900 July call at 25¢ and long the WMC 1000 July put at 12¢. The total outlay for this strategy was 37¢. A combination had been created.

The advantage of this can be seen in the following scenarios. If WMC continued to rise to $10.00 by expiry, the call would be worth $1.00 and the put would expire worthless, a total profit of 63¢, ($1 profit on the call minus the 25¢ price of the call option minus the 12¢ price of the put). If WMC fell back towards $9.00 at expiry, the call would expire worthless and the put would be worth $1.00, again a total profit of 63¢. If WMC finished at $9.50 the call would be worth 50¢ and the put would be worth 50¢ — again a net profit of 63¢.

If WMC finished anywhere between $9.00 and $10.00 at expiry, a net profit of 63¢ would be available to our trader. Similarly, if WMC either fell below $9.00 or rose above $10.00, the position would be worth more than $1.00.

Thus we have created a position where we cannot lose money. We paid 37¢ to put the combination in place and irrespective of where WMC finishes, the strategy will always be worth at least $1.00 at expiry — a net profit of 63¢ has been locked in. However, before the reader gets over-excited about the possibility of being able to create an endless series of no-loss situations, remember that this situation arose from what was initially a call buying strategy only.

This combination was created as a fall-back position in order to lock in an unrealised profit. This type of strategy is a follow-up to either a successful call or put purchase, it is not an initial position. The market does not work that way.

To demonstrate an initial position, let's assume the following situation exists:

EXAMPLE

RIO is trading at $22.00. We purchase a combination by buying a 2250 September call and a 2150 September put for say 75¢ and 45¢ respectively. Notice how both the put and the call are out-of-the-money. For a range of possible outcomes see Table 6.1.

The maximum loss on this strategy is possible over a very wide range — if the stock does not move by a large amount by expiry then losses will be incurred. The maximum loss will occur if the stock is between the two strike prices at expiry.

Table 6.1 Possible Outcomes

RIO at Expiry	2250 Call Value	Profit/ loss	2150 Put Value	Profit/ loss	Total Profit/ loss
1850	0	-75	300	+255	+180
1900	0	-75	250	+205	+130
1950	0	-75	200	+155	+80
2000	0	-75	150	+105	+30
2050	0	-75	100	+55	-20
2100	0	-75	50	+5	-70
2150	0	-75	0	-45	-120
2200	0	-75	0	-45	-120
2250	0	-75	0	-45	-120
2300	50	-25	0	-45	-70
2350	100	+25	0	-45	-20
2400	150	+75	0	-45	+30

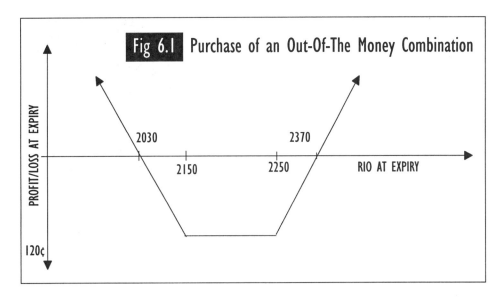

Fig 6.1 Purchase of an Out-Of-The Money Combination

As a further example, let's reverse the situation. Assume that we purchase a 2250 put and a 2150 call. Since both options are in-the-money, our outlay will be higher so assume the purchase prices are 50¢ and $1.00 respectively. Total outlay is therefore $1.50. Table 6.2 and Fig. 6.2 show what is possible.

Table 6.2 Possible Outcomes

RIO at Expiry	2150 Call Value	Profit/ loss	2250 Put Value	Profit/ loss	Total Profit/ loss
1850	0	-100	400	+350	+250
1900	0	-100	350	+300	+200
1950	0	-100	300	+250	+150
2000	0	-100	250	+200	+100
2050	0	-100	200	+150	+50
2100	0	-100	150	+100	0
2150	0	-100	100	+50	-50
2200	50	-50	50	0	-50
2250	100	0	0	-50	-50
2300	150	+50	0	-50	0
2350	200	+100	0	-50	+50
2400	250	+150	0	-50	+100

Our strategy will incur its maximum loss if our stock is between the strike prices at expiry. Even though this strategy cost more to initially establish it is superior to our out-of-the-money since our maximum loss is lower. It should be noted that in both strategies the maximum loss occurred between our two strike prices. Being long both the put and the call requires the underlying stock to move beyond the strike price plus the cost of the option for us to be profitable.

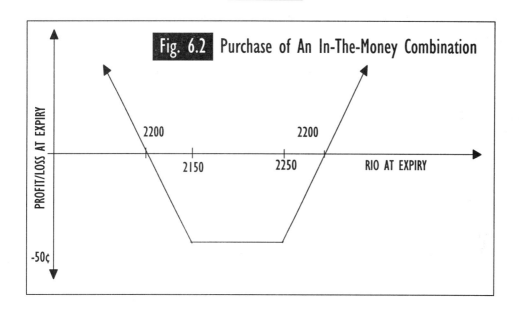

Fig. 6.2 Purchase of An In-The-Money Combination

THE WRITTEN COMBINATION

The written combination is more often referred to as the "strangle" — the objective being to squeeze the stock between two strike prices. In setting up a strangle, you are effectively writing both a naked call and naked put.

Just as our earlier discussion on combinations distinguished between using in-the-money and out-of-the money options, so will our discussion on strangles.

It is my opinion that because of the risks involved, traders should, unless they are very aggressive, avoid writing in-the-money strangles. To reinforce this, let's refer back to our in-the-money combination. In this instance we were long the RIO 2250 September put at 50¢ and long the RIO 2150 September call at $1.00, and both options were in-the-money. If we had sold this strangle, we would have received $1.50 in premium income. However, what are the risks involved? Assume we had to buy our position back at expiry, Table 6.3 and Table 6.4 show what is likely.

If we refer back to our example of an in-the-money combination, we can see that the zone of maximum loss occurs between the two option strike prices; in the sold situation the reverse is true, this is our zone of maximum profit. Any result outside this band sees us in a loss situation.

Table 6.3 Possible Outcomes

RIO at Expiry	2150 Call Value	Profit/ loss	2250 Put Value	Profit/ loss	Total Profit/ loss
1850	0	+100	400	-350	-250
1900	0	+100	350	-300	-200
1950	0	+100	300	-250	-150
2000	0	+100	250	-200	-100
2050	0	+100	200	-150	-50
2100	0	+100	150	-100	0
2150	0	+100	100	-50	+50
2200	50	+50	50	0	+50
2250	100	0	0	+50	+50
2300	150	-50	0	+50	0
2350	200	-100	0	+50	-50
2400	250	-150	0	+50	-100

The large premium income makes this strategy appear attractive; however, Table 6.4 shows the possibilities at each expiry price.

The large premium income received is compensation for the risk we take in writing naked options. Remember that, in writing a put option, we have obligated ourselves to buy a given stock at what may be a price higher than the prevailing market price, and by writing a call we have obligated ourselves to sell a stock at a price that may be much lower than the market price.

It should also be remembered that to undertake this strategy we would have to conform to the OCH's requirements for margins and deposits. This, however, is never a reason not to undertake a strategy.

This is a most aggressive strategy and should not be undertaken by any trader who does not understand the risks involved. Our downside risk is that our put may be exercised and we would have to take on stock at a premium to the market. The upside risk is that our call would be exercised and we would have to deliver stock at a discount to the market.

If traders do take this position, they must carefully define their breakeven points and have an adequate knowledge of what sort of defensive action is available to them. Be warned that in a quickly moving market, options may move through breakeven points very rapidly or, on the downside, your put may be exercised before you have a chance to close it out — either way, it may be an expensive exercise.

A more conservative trader may seek to sell out-of-the-money options for a lower premium income and consequently lower risk. Such a situation may arise where a

Table 6.4 Possible Outcomes

RIO at Expiry	Outcome
1850	Put exercise
1900	Put exercise
1950	Put exercise
2000	Put exercise
2050	Put exercise
2100	Put exercise
2150	Put/call exercise
2200	Put/call exercise
2250	Put/call exercise
2300	Call exercise
2350	Call exercise
2400	Call exercise

conservative trader wishes to strangle STO which is trading at $5.25. In this situation it may be possible to sell an STO 475 June put for 15¢, and an STO 550 June call for 30¢; our total premium income is therefore 45¢. Hence, our downside breakeven point is $4.30, i.e. 475 - 45¢, and our upside breakeven is $5.95, i.e. 550 + 45¢.

The ideal result would be for STO to finish somewhere between $4.75 and $5.50 at expiry, hence both our options would expire worthless.

In comparison to the in-the-money strangle, we have a broad range before one leg of our strategy becomes in-the-money. With an in-the-money strangle, no matter where the stock moves one leg is always in-the-money.

Although often rejected because of margin and deposit requirements and perceived risk in a flat or mildly trending market, the strangle is one of the most effective strategies available to traders.

THE STRADDLE

The straddle may be defined as the simultaneous purchase of an equal number of puts and calls that have the same underlying stock, strike price and expiry month. The basic idea in buying a straddle is that the trader perceives that a particular stock will break strongly in a given direction, either up or down, yet the direction of this break is uncertain. Such a situation may occur when a stock approaches a traditional line of resistance — it may either breach this resistance or retreat from it. So for a predetermined outlay, the trader may participate in any movement in the stock.

Like all option buying strategies, the loss is limited to our initial investment and our potential profit is unlimited. As an example, assume that the following prices exist:

EXAMPLE

MIM is trading at $2.20
MIM 225 July call is trading at 16¢
MIM 225 July put is trading at 14¢

If we bought both the July 225 call and the July 225 put, we would own a straddle, the cost of which is 30¢. Table 6.5 and Fig. 6.3 show the range of possible outcomes.

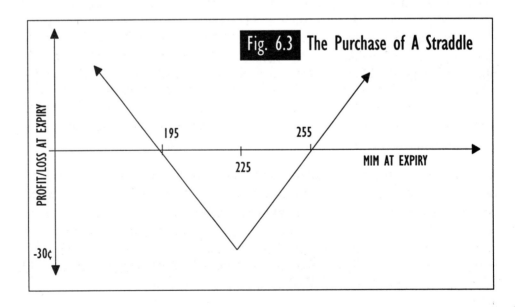

Fig. 6.3 The Purchase of A Straddle

PROFIT/LOSS AT EXPIRY

195   255

225

MIM AT EXPIRY

-30¢

Table 6.5 Range of Possible Outcomes

MIM at Expiry	225 Put Value	Profit/ loss	225 Call Value	Profit/ loss	Total Profit/ loss
175	50	+36	0	-16	+20
185	40	+26	0	-16	+10
195	30	+16	0	-16	0
205	20	+6	0	-16	-10
215	10	-4	0	-16	-20
225	0	-14	0	-16	-30
235	0	-14	10	-6	-20
245	0	-14	20	+4	-10
255	0	-14	30	+14	0
265	0	-14	40	+24	+10
275	0	-14	50	+34	+20

Notice how there is a direct relationship between our breakeven point and our initial outlay. In this example, our initial outlay was 30¢, therefore, our breakeven range is defined as being the strike price of the option plus or minus our initial debit, i.e. 225 + 30¢ = 255 and 225 - 30¢ = 195. Thus, our breakeven range is between $1.95 and $2.55; if MIM is not outside this band by expiry, we will lose money. If MIM is at exactly $2.25 (an unlikely event) then the possibility exists to lose our total investment.

Straddles are generally only suitable for volatile stocks that have a capacity to move far enough during the limited life of our option. In this example, MIM had to move some 30¢ or 13 per cent in either direction for the play to be profitable. Such a need to move in large amounts often renders the straddle an inappropriate strategy for the Australian market where the underlying option stocks may not display the necessary inherent volatility to make the play profitable. However, it may be considered when option premiums are very low and the initial outlay is quite small, thereby narrowing the breakeven points. If the premiums are low, then a trader may take a position in a stock via a cheap straddle — the bulk of his investment capital may then be placed in a cash instrument. If the strategy works, then there is a chance of a windfall gain. If not, then the straddle can be sold to recoup funds and the interest earned by holding the bulk of the investment in cash will help offset any loss on the straddle.

By now, the reader has probably realised that any option strategy that can be bought, i.e. is a long position, may be sold or written. This is true for both combinations and straddles.

THE WRITTEN STRADDLE

The written straddle is in many ways analogous to the strangle — the major difference is that we narrow our focus to one strike price. Just as a bought strategy can be implemented by a trader anticipating a sharp movement, conversely a written straddle is created where such a movement may not be expected. For example, let's assume the following prices:

EXAMPLE

CSR is trading at $5.00
CSR 500 June call is trading at 29¢
CSR 500 June put is trading at 22¢

A straddle can be sold for 51¢; if CSR is between $4.49 and $5.51 at expiry then we will realise a profit. This is shown in Fig. 6.4 and Table 6.6.

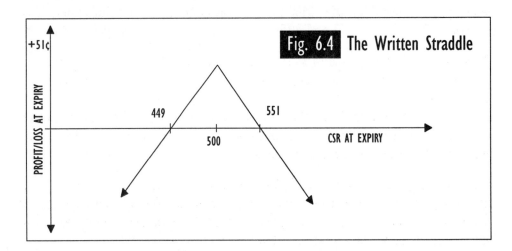

Fig. 6.4 The Written Straddle

Table 6.6 Possible Outcomes

CSR at Expiry	500 Call Value	Profit/ loss	500 Put Value	Profit/ loss	Total Profit/ loss
425	0	+29	75	-53	-24
450	0	+29	50	-28	+1
475	0	+29	25	-3	+26
500	0	+29	0	+22	+51
525	25	+4	0	+22	+26
550	50	-21	0	+22	+1
575	75	-46	0	+22	-24
600	100	-71	0	+22	-49

Our maximum profit potential is achieved if CSR finishes at the strike price at expiry and a large potential for losses exists if the stock moves too far in either direction. For this reason, it is imperative that a trader be well versed in the potential risks of such a strategy, such as large price fluctuations and the possibility of being exercised, since one leg of the play is always in-the-money unless the stock remains at the exercise price for the duration of the option. Before putting a sold straddle in place, we should be aware of possible defensive actions.

There are several fall-back positions available if a straddle goes wrong. Firstly, we may simply buy the straddle back; we would never buy back both legs since it is impossible for both sides of the straddle to go wrong simultaneously. This may be an effective strategy if we had to buy our put back, since, as has been noted before, put options lose time value very quickly once they are in-the-money. So we may be able to close this leg with minimal losses.

If the market is very bullish and we have to take action to close out the call leg, this may prove to be expensive since the time value of a call option may not shrink by much at all. Hence, buying back a straddle is much more effective in the latter stages of an option's life since their time value decays rapidly.

A refinement of this involves the concept of "rolling" which was introduced earlier.

If CSR fell dramatically, our 500 put would be in-the-money. To keep the position alive we would close out the 500 put and roll into a lower strike. If our indicators pointed to continued weakness in CSR's price, we may even decide on a two-pronged defence based upon not only rolling down our put but also rolling down our call. Whilst this preserves the straddle, it is a very aggressive response and not for the faint-hearted. If we were to only roll down our put then we would have converted our play from a straddle to a strangle.

Similarly, if CSR broke strongly upwards, we would consider rolling up our call to a higher strike price. The philosophy behind rolling is to keep a strategy alive and to always do so with a net credit. If your particular strategy can be implemented without a debit transaction, then go ahead and do so. Always remember the old adage that it is better to get a start than to give one!

Fig 6.5 Puts & Calls Together Summary

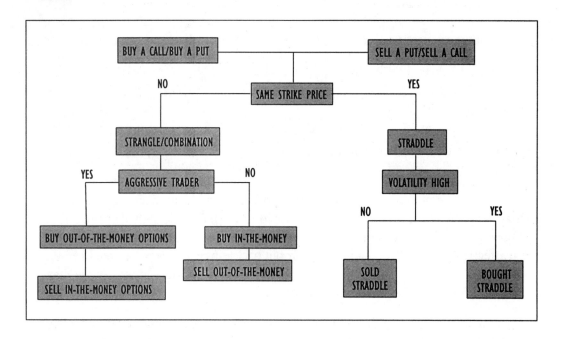

SPREADS

Chapter Seven

A spread is created with the simultaneous buying and selling of options of the same underlying security but with differing strike prices. Spreads are amongst the most popular strategies available to options traders. The basic technique of creating spreads was briefly touched upon in earlier chapters. Spreads can be either bullish or bearish in their outlook; likewise they may be created by using either calls or puts. Hence, we can have call and put bull spreads and call and put bear spreads.

BULL SPREADS

CALL BULL SPREADS

A call bull spread is created by buying a low strike price call and selling a higher strike price call. Assume the following option prices:

EXAMPLE

CBA is trading at $14.50
Oct 1450 call is trading at 55¢
Oct 1500 call is trading at 30¢

If we were to buy the CBA 1450 Oct call at 55¢ and sell the CBA 1500 Oct call at 30¢, then we would have created a bull spread. Note that this is a debit transaction — it costs us money to set up.

A bull spread is profitable if the stock moves up in price; the spread has limited profit potential and limited risk.

Table 7.1 shows a range of possible outcomes at expiry.

Table 7.1 Possible Outcomes

CBA at Expiry	1450 Call Value	Profit/ loss	1500 Call Value	Profit/ loss	Total Profit/ loss
1400	0	-55	0	+30	-25
1425	0	-55	0	+30	-25
1450	0	-55	0	+30	-25
1475	25	-30	0	+30	0
1500	50	-5	0	+30	+25
1525	75	+20	25	+5	+25
1550	100	+45	50	-20	+25
1575	125	+70	75	-45	+25
1600	150	+95	100	-70	+25
1625	175	+120	125	-95	+25
1650	200	+145	150	-120	+25

Several points are evident; firstly, our maximum profit is realised if the stock finishes at or above the higher strike price and secondly, a maximum loss is incurred if the stock is below the lower strike price.

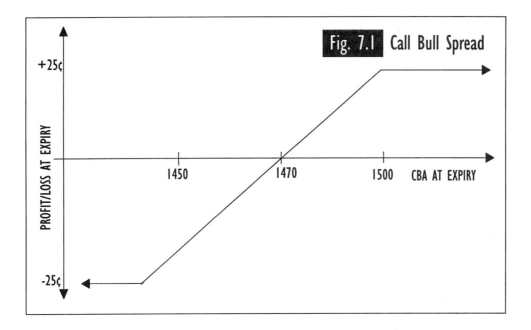

Fig. 7.1 Call Bull Spread

As with all strategies, a breakeven point can be easily defined. In this instance, it is the lower strike price plus the net debit of the spread. Hence, breakeven is:

$$1450 + 25 = 1475¢.$$

The reader will already have realised that this is not an overwhelmingly bullish play since we have limited our risk at the expense of our maximum potential profit. If a trader was very aggressive, he would purchase the lower strike price by itself, and naturally such a strategy would outperform the bull spread if the stock moved up sharply.

PUT BULL SPREADS

A put bull spread is established by buying a put at a lower strike price and selling a put at a higher strike price. Note that this is exactly the same way we established a call bull spread. To illustrate the construction of such a spread, consider the following prices.

If we buy the June 1400 put and sell the June 1450 put, we have again created a bull spread. Unlike the call bull spread this is a credit

EXAMPLE

CBA is trading at $14.50
CBA 1400 put is trading at 50¢
CBA 1450 put is trading at 70¢

transaction, in this example the credit is 10¢. Table 7.2 and Fig. 7.2 show possible outcomes at expiry:

Table 7.2 Possible Outcomes

CBA at Expiry	1400 Put Value	Profit/ loss	1450 Put Value	Profit/ loss	Total Profit/ loss
1275	125	+75	175	-105	-30
1300	100	+50	150	-80	-30
1325	75	+25	125	-55	-30
1350	50	0	100	-30	-30
1375	25	-25	75	-5	-30
1400	0	-50	50	+20	-30
1425	0	-50	25	+45	-5
1450	0	-50	0	+70	+20
1475	0	-50	0	+70	+20
1500	0	-50	0	+70	+20
1525	0	-50	0	+70	+20
1550	0	-50	0	+70	+20

In this instance, our maximum profit is restricted to our initial credit of 20¢ and the maximum loss occurs if our stock is anywhere below our lower strike price at expiry.

The breakeven point of this type of strategy is equal to the higher strike price minus net credit. Thus, in this example, our breakeven = 1450 - 20 = 1430¢.

In general, call bull spreads are superior to put bull spreads. The major disadvantage with put bull spreads is that we are selling an in-the-money put which may be subject to early exercise which would render the strategy unprofitable. A call bull spread's short position is not in-the-money till the strategy has passed its point of maximum potential profit.

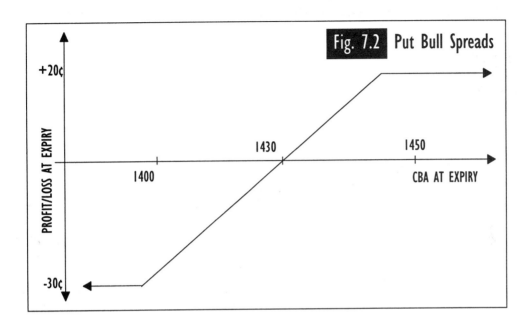

Fig. 7.2 Put Bull Spreads

BEAR SPREADS

CALL BEAR SPREADS

A call bear spread is created by selling a lower strike price call and buying a higher strike price call — this is the reverse of how we established a call bull spread. As such, the strategy is profitable if the underlying stock declines in value.

To illustrate the construction of a call bear spread, let's use the following values:

EXAMPLE

NAB is trading at $18.75
NAB Oct 1800 call is trading at $1.00
NAB Oct 1850 call is trading at 85¢

If we sell the Oct 1800 call at $1.00 and buy the Oct 1850 call at 85¢, we have created a call bear spread, because we have sold the lower strike price call; this is a credit transaction. In this example, the credit is 15¢ which represents our maximum potential profit which would be realised if NAB dropped sharply and both calls expired worthless.

To illustrate this point, consider the following range of outcomes.

Table 7.3 Possible Outcomes

NAB at Expiry	1800 Call Value	Profit/ loss	1850 Call Value	Profit/ loss	Total Profit/ loss
1650	0	+100	0	-85	+15
1675	0	+100	0	-85	+15
1700	0	+100	0	-85	+15
1725	0	+100	0	-85	+15
1750	0	+100	0	-85	+15
1775	0	+100	0	-85	+15
1800	0	+100	0	-85	+15
1825	25	+75	0	-85	-10
1850	50	+50	0	-85	-35
1875	75	+25	25	-60	-35
1900	100	0	50	-35	-35
1925	125	-25	75	-10	-35
1950	150	-50	100	+15	-35
1975	175	-75	125	+40	-35
2000	200	-100	150	+65	-35

This range of outcomes is exactly the opposite of those possible for a call bull spread. Our maximum profit is limited to our initial credit and the maximum potential loss is 35¢ which is the difference between the two strike prices less the initial credit we received. The breakeven point on this strategy can be defined as being the lower strike price plus the initial credit received, i.e. 1800 + 15 = 1815¢.

PUT BEAR SPREADS

A put bear spread is established by selling a put at a lower strike price and buying a put with a higher strike price. Once again, this is the opposite way to which we would have constructed a bull spread using puts.

As an example, let's use the following prices:

EXAMPLE

STO is trading at $4.20
STO May 400 put is trading at 10¢
STO May 425 put is trading at 20¢

To construct a put bear spread we would buy the May 425 put and sell the May 400 put. Such a transaction would cost us approximately 10¢. To illustrate what happens at expiry, consider Table 7.4 and Fig. 7.3.

Table 7.4 Possible Outcomes

STO at Expiry	400 Put Value	Profit/ loss	425 Put Value	Profit/ loss	Total Profit/ loss
350	50	-40	75	+55	+15
375	25	-15	50	+30	+15
400	0	+10	25	+5	+15
425	0	+10	0	-20	-10
450	0	+10	0	-20	-10
475	0	+10	0	-20	-10
500	0	+10	0	-20	-10

Again our range of outcomes is the reverse of that possible with a put bull spread. Our maximum loss is limited to our initial debit of 10¢ and our maximum profit potential is the difference between the two strike prices minus our initial debit, i.e. 15¢. Our breakeven point is once again defined as the higher strike price minus the initial debit, i.e. 425 - 10 = 415¢.

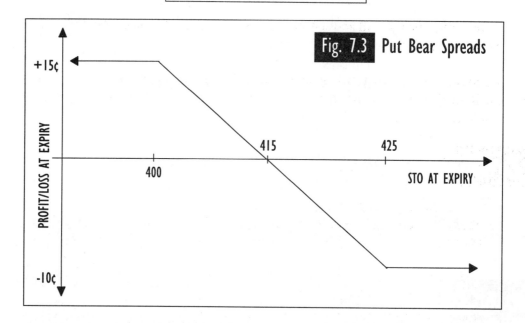

Fig. 7.3 Put Bear Spreads

Just as our optimum way to construct a bull spread was to use calls, the most efficient way to construct a bear spread is to use puts. This is because when constructing a bear spread using calls we are selling an in-the-money call and buying an out-of-the-money call. The result of this is that we are buying more time value than we are selling and this is the opposite to what we would generally like to achieve. The idea of selling calls is to sell those with high time values and let the natural time decay effect quickly reduce the value of the call. There is also the additional consideration that in selling an in-the-money call, there is always the chance of being exercised before the spread is profitable.

RATIO SPREADS

The spread strategies outlined, as well as having exactly the same expiry dates, also had a constant ratio of options bought and sold. For each option bought one was sold; hence, a ratio of 1:1 was established. Such a ratio is not mandatory in constructing a spread.

Consider the following example.

If we were to buy the 600 call and sell the 650 call, we would have constructed a standard bull spread. However, as a variation, if we

EXAMPLE

NCP is trading at $6
NCP Nov 600 call is trading at 60¢
NCP Nov 650 call is trading at 34¢

were to buy one 600 call and sell two 650, we would have created a ratio spread. Such a strategy would yield a credit of 8¢.

Ratio spreads are most efficient when established for an initial credit since there is no downside risk. Upon expiry, the following possible outcomes are shown in Table 7.5 and Fig. 7.4.

Table 7.5 Possible Outcomes

NCP Expiry	600 Call Value	Profit/ loss	650 Call Value	Profit/ loss	x2	Total Profit/ loss
500	0	-60	0	+34	+68	+8
525	0	-60	0	+34	+68	+8
550	0	-60	0	+34	+68	+8
575	0	-60	0	+34	+68	+8
600	0	-60	0	+34	+68	+8
625	25	-35	0	+34	+68	+33
650	50	-10	0	+34	+68	+58
675	75	+15	25	+9	+18	+33
700	100	+40	50	-16	-32	+8
725	125	+65	75	-41	-82	-17
750	150	+90	100	-66	-132	-42
775	175	+115	125	-91	-182	-67
800	200	+140	150	-116	-232	-92

In ratio spreads, there is no downside risk; the risk in the strategy is on the upside where losses can be unlimited as with all naked option strategies.

The point of maximum profit for this strategy was 650. This is self-evident because if NCP finished at $6.50, our 600 call would be worth 50¢ and our 650 position would expire worthless. Thus, we would pocket 58¢. The breakeven point on the upside is our maximum profit, 58¢ plus the higher strike price 650, i.e. 708¢.

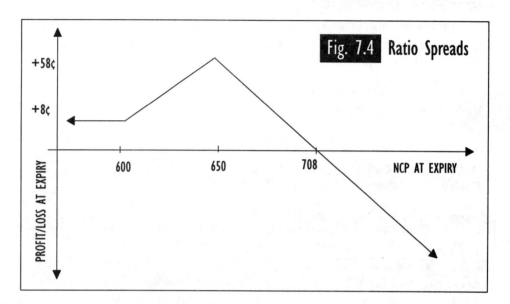

Since this strategy has a good probability of making a profit with no downside risk, it is one traders should be familiar with. The strategy is very effective when a 2:1 ratio is employed. However, the more aggressive trader may choose a 3:1 ratio to establish a credit position. In fact, this may more often be the case since the efficiency with which the market prices options may make establishing a credit with a 2:1 ratio impossible. However, it is not common to establish a ratio of greater than 4:1 due to the large increase in the upside risk associated with such high ratios.

MORE ADVANCED SPREADS

All the examples of spreads we have dealt with so far have had one element in common: the options from which they were constructed all had the same expiry date. Spreads constructed from options that have the same expiry date are known as vertical spreads. Common strike prices are not a prerequisite for the creation of a spread. A spread that depends on the sale of one option and the purchase of another option of a different expiry date is known as a calendar spread.

HORIZONTAL CALENDAR SPREAD

Suppose the following prices exist in April:

> WMC is trading at $10.00

We review the available options and note the following:

> WMC May 1000 call is trading at 50¢   WMC Aug 1000 call is trading at 75¢

If we were to sell the May 1000 call and buy the August 1000 call for a net cost of 25¢, we would have created a calendar spread.

Suppose that by May WMC is relatively unchanged in price, then our May 1000 call will expire worthless and our August 1000 call should be worth approximately 50¢. Initially, we have established a spread at a cost of 25¢ and by May our spread is worth 50¢. The August 1000 call can be sold for 50¢ and we would have made a profit of 25¢.

If WMC had dropped sharply, then our risk is limited to our initial debit of 25¢. This is also true if WMC had risen sharply before expiry. Note also that we have protected ourselves against the possibility of exercise by having a long position. If we were to be exercised, we would in turn satisfy delivery requirements by exercising our long position.

The overall aim in setting up calendar spreads is that we are selling time. Our rationale is based on the fact that a near-term option will lose time value more quickly than a long-dated option.

THE DIAGONAL CALENDAR SPREAD

If a trader makes use, not only of different strike prices, but also differing expiry dates, then a diagonal spread is created.

To illustrate how a variety of spreads can be constructed, assume the following prices exist:

WMC is trading at $10.00

STRIKE PRICE	MAY	AUGUST	NOVEMBER
1000	40¢	75¢	95¢
1100	20¢	45¢	55¢

To create a standard bull spread, we would buy the May 1000 call and sell the May 1100 call. To create a calendar spread, we would sell the May 1000 and buy the August 1000. To establish a diagonal calendar bull spread, we would buy the August 1000 and sell the May 1100 call for a debit of 55¢.

Whilst the diagonal calendar spread is more expensive to implement than a standard bull spread, it re-orientates the spread on the downward side. The slightly lower profit potential also means that the probability of total loss is lowered. If the stock falls suddenly, the longer-term call would retain some value because of its greater time to maturity.

Fig. 7.7   Spreads

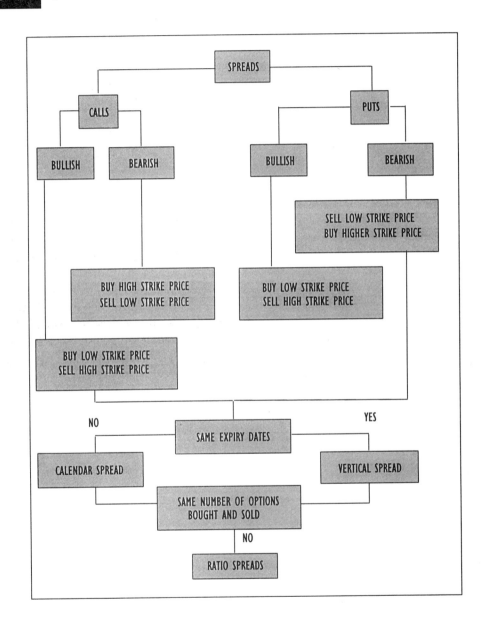

WARRANTS AND LEPO TRADING

Since the publication of the first edition of this book there has been an enormous growth in the trading of warrants. Traders have seen that warrants offer many of the advantages in terms of speculation, leverage and protection that Exchange Traded Options (ETOs) possess. Whilst not strictly ETOs, warrants are worth examining because they do share some similarities with options and they add flexibility to the trader's arsenal.

A warrant can be defined as an option that has been issued by a financial institution such as a merchant bank. A range of institutions may issue warrants for trading. Institutions that can issue warrants include Australian banks, the government, a merchant bank or any group that is deemed by the Australian

Stock Exchange (ASX) to have the necessary financial backing, knowledge of securities and experience. Examples of warrant issuers in the Australian market include:

> Macquarie Bank LTD   >   BT Australia LTD

> Deutsche Bank AG   >   SBC Warburg Australia Ltd.

In issuing a warrant an institution has certain responsibilities such as maintaining a register of warrant holders and maintaining a presence in the market on both the buy and sell side. In this instance the issuer acts to a degree like a Registered Trader (RT) in that it provides a bid with an offer. Although as the depth of the secondary market has grown liquidity is not a problem as it was when warrants were first listed.

I must admit I was initially critical of warrants as just another financial product squeezed into an already crowded market and for some time they had little liquidity and there was little reason to trade them. However as traders have become more familiar with warrants, and the overall market has picked up, the liquidity in warrants has soared.

Unlike ETOs which are traded by an open outcry system on the trading floor, warrants are traded on the ASX via the Stock Exchange Automated Trading System (SEATS). In my opinion this is the single most valuable feature of warrants now that liquidity has increased. SEATS brings an ease of trading to warrants that is missing from the options market and there are times that because of this I prefer to deal in warrants

Warrants, like ETOs, may be either put or call warrants. A call warrant gives the holder the right to *buy* the underlying asset at a fixed price on or before the expiry date. A put warrant enables the holder to *sell* the underlying asset at a fixed price on or before the expiry date. Note, most warrants are American-style options, they can be exercised at any time during the life of an option.

However, there are some major differences between warrants and ETOs, apart from them being traded via SEATS.

> *You cannot short sell a warrant.* It may sound obvious that the only instance in which a warrant holder may sell a warrant is if he already holds that particular warrant. This is an unfortunate drawback but one which cannot be overcome due to the fundamental nature of the warrant.

> *Warrant issuers do not have to pay margins throughout the life of the warrant.* However, should a warrant holder seek to exercise his warrant, then

the issuer must in the case of a call warrant sell the underlying instrument to the holder at the terms under which the warrant was issued. Or in the case of a put warrant buy the underlying instrument. The obligations of a warrant issuer are in this respect analogous to someone who has written or sold an option. It should also be noted that some warrants may be settled in cash. A situation that has no corollary in the trading of ETOs.

> *Warrants also have no fixed expiry cycle like ETOs.* In many instances, at the time of issue their expiry date may be several years away, a distinct advantage in a lot of situations. It is this longer life span that gives warrants an advantage over options when traders are seeking to have a synthetic share portfolio. For instance, instead of buying BHP, CBA, WMC and LLC I may elect to buy long-dated equity warrants instead.

It is important to understand that warrants come in a variety of types and these are detailed below. Although complete details of the terms and conditions of each warrant can only be obtained from your stockbroker and from a copy of the original offer documents.

EQUITY WARRANTS

These are the easiest warrants to understand. They are issued as either puts or calls over an underlying share. So, like ETOs, they give the holder the right to buy or sell the underlying share at a fixed price throughout the life of the option contract. As an example the warrant which has the ASX code PASWBT is an equity warrant that gives the holder the right to buy Pasminco at $2.00 at any time on or before the expiry date of 23 April 1998. Equity warrants are an excellent tool for traders because they allow a leveraged exposure to the underlying share without the complications that are incurred in other warrants. As such, equity warrants can serve as replacements for similar ETOs.

FRACTIONAL WARRANTS

Fractional warrants are similar in most respects to standard equity warrants. However, in the case of a fractional warrant, a number of warrants are required to be exercised per underlying share. For example CBAWDA is a warrant issued by Deutsche Bank AG with an exercise price of $5.25 and an expiry date of 25 December 1997. The difference between this and similar CBA warrants is that CBAWDA requires two warrants to be exercised to acquire the underlying stock.

INDEX WARRANTS

Index warrants are simply warrants over a given index such as the banking or mining index. In this instance the value of the warrant is calculated by applying an appropriate multiplier per point of the index. Such warrants are cash settled. My own personal experience is that these warrants came into being during a time of friction between the ASX and the Sydney Futures Exchange (SFE). A cynic might suggest that they were an attempt by the ASX to take business away from the SFE by offering a product that was analogous to the Share Price Index contract offered by the SFE. Index warrants did not turn out to be the great success that was hoped for and at the time of writing there are no index warrants listed on the ASX.

BASKET WARRANTS

As the name implies such warrants are issued over a group of shares that often carry out similar activities or are members of the same indices. For example a basket warrant may cover a varying ratio of ANZ, CBA, NAB and WBC bank shares. This would enable me to form a view on an industry sector. If I were bullish the banking system I may buy the basket warrant as a substitute for trading individual equity warrants over each bank. To date basket warrants have not been a great success.

INSTALMENT WARRANTS

An instalment warrant is similar to a standard equity warrant but with the difference that the warrant holder is entitled to any dividends along with franking credits that are paid by the underlying share. Instalment warrants are similar to partly paid shares in that to convert to fully paid ordinary shares a second instalment is due.

ENDOWMENT WARRANTS

Endowment warrants are an intriguing concept. They are different from standard equity warrants in that they have no fixed exercise date and are European in nature. They work by having what is referred to as an "outstanding amount" which changes over the life of the warrant. The outstanding amount is determined by the issuer of the warrant at the time of the warrants' creation. In effect, the trader pays a deposit on the warrant of anywhere between 30 per cent to 60 per cent and over the life of the warrant the outstanding amount is reduced by the payment of dividends from the shares. Once the outstanding amount is paid, the trader becomes the owner of the shares with no more financial commitments. The warrant holder can also elect to pay the outstanding amount during the life of the warrant thereby receiving ownership of the shares before the expiry date.

Sounds too good to be true, merely put a deposit on the shares and the dividends pay off the balance. As one broker trumpets in their sales blurb, a solid investment decision, no maintenance equity investment.

Unfortunately the world doesn't work that way. When an endowment warrant is created an interest rate is applied to it which is applied to the balance outstanding. So if you were to purchase CBAWCE, an endowment warrant over CBA, that had a balance outstanding when issued of 6.137 per cent (floating), then you are in a race to see whether the dividends cover the interest payments. The interest rate is defined as the 180 day bank bill swap rate, so this is a floating rate. There is a cut-off date for the endowment warrants after which the issuer can request the warrant holder to pay the outstanding amount or forfeit the warrant.

To place such a vehicle in context you must view the most negative of scenarios. Assume you have purchased one of these warrants with the view to having the maturity coincide with your retirement. Your plan is based on the premise that the option has, say, 10 years to maturity and that is approximately the length of time until you retire. It is your thought that 10 years would be more than sufficient for the dividend stream to pay off the outstanding amount. However, let's assume that we encounter a five-year period of high interest rates (such periods occur with regularity) and the interest rate on your warrant accelerates to 15 per cent. Under such a scenario, the dividend stream cannot keep pace with the outstanding amount and you arrive at retirement facing the prospect of having to pay a substantial outstanding amount.

HINTS FOR TRADING WARRANTS

Before beginning an exploration of some of the basic mechanics of warrants trading I need to revisit a sentiment that was the central theme of many of the sections on options trading.

If you cannot successfully trade shares then you WILL NOT be able to trade warrants.

All warrants will enable you to do is to lose your money in a more creative and faster manner. Warrants will not save you from having no ability as a trader. If you have not taken time to research and design a trading method, learn about the importance of money management or understand the role of your own psychology in the trading process then it will be impossible for you to make money. Forget about the stories you hear of amateurs making fortunes in bull markets. Firstly, most such stories are exaggerated. Secondly, anybody can make some money in a bull market.

As with options trading the first step in trading a given warrant revolves around the selection of the underlying share. Only by understanding the price action of the underlying share will you begin to understand the potential for profit via trading that particular company's warrants. This reinforces my earlier blunt point about being able to trade shares effectively. If you cannot make a reasoned judgment about the probable movement of the underlying share then it will be impossible for you to translate this inability into profitable warrants trading.

If you find that you are continually wrong in your analysis of the underlying share and its market direction, then you have to work on the points I outlined earlier with regard to designing a trading system.

Your view on the stock is then translated into a positive or negative expectation. Negative expectations would cause you to look at the put or short side of the market. A positive expectation would cause you to look at the call or long side of the market. If at this point you are tripping over terminology such as long, short, put or call, go back to the beginning of this book and start again.

Merely having a view on the stock is only a fraction of the decision-making process. You do not, for example, decide BHP is going up and then buy the first call option you see listed in the financial press. Remember warrants, like options, are time-dependent securities. They have a limited life and time dramatically influences their performance and your capacity to be profitable. For example, it would be pointless viewing NAB on a monthly basis and then buying a warrant with only three weeks to expiry. Your view must have a time component to it. Sitting on a warrant wishing and hoping for something to happen is not a trading strategy.

It is at this stage in the selection process that the concept of gearing comes into the selection criteria. Gearing is expressed as a multiple; the higher the multiple the higher your return or losses will be. Gearing is an integral part of the risk/reward equation; the higher the potential return the greater the potential downside risk. This is one of the universal constants in trading.

The final selection criteria is a make or break hurdle. If a warrant has no turnover DO NOT under any circumstances purchase it. Volume is the driving force in the market and it is the key to the successful trading of any instrument. The rule for volume is simple; *No volume, no trade.* Ignore this rule at your peril. I have literally lost count of the number of times I have seen traders buy a warrant and then not be able to sell it at a reasonable market price. Forget all the nonsense you hear about the issuer of the warrant being obliged to make a market. Often they don't, and if they do the market they make will not be to your advantage. Being a market maker is not a public service activity; they are in the game to make money the same as you are, and the only way they can make money is if you lose.

BARRIER WARRANTS

Barrier warrants are one of the newer breed of warrants appearing in the late 1990s. A barrier warrant is simply a standard warrant that has an enforced upper or lower limit. This barrier imposes a trading range upon the warrant. If the warrant closes beyond the barrier for a predetermined number of trading days, it expires, irrespective of how much time is left till the stated expiry date.

For example, let's assume we had a barrier call warrant on the All Ordinaries Index. Let's assume that this warrant had an expiry date of October 1999 and a barrier limit of 3200 — that is, if the All Ordinaries closed above 3200 the barrier would be terminated and the option would expire on that day. It does not matter whether the barrier is triggered one year, one month or one day before expiry. Once it is breached then the warrant is terminated. The consequences of the barrier for the trader are two-fold. Firstly, the establishment of the trading range can limit the potential for upside in a given trade. Secondly, it introduces another variable into the trading equation that traders need to be aware of.

CURRENCY WARRANTS

Currency warrants entitle the holder of the warrant to exchange an amount of a foreign currency for an equivalent amount in Australian dollars. As you would expect, as the value of the Australian dollar rises and falls so too would the value of respective warrants.

If you had an A$/US$ call warrant then a rise in the Australian dollar will see an increase in the value of the warrant. A decay in the exchange rate would see this warrant decrease in value and an increase in the value of any put warrants.

RISKS IN WARRANT TRADING

Just as there are risks in trading ETOs there are also risks in trading warrants. If you cannot trade shares successfully, then you will simply transfer your lack of success to trading warrants. This is a problem that is faced by all market participants and is beyond the scope of this book to address. However, there are some structural problems that warrant traders may face.

The prime risk faced by a warrant trader is that the issuer may go belly up and not meet its obligations in terms of delivery. The purchase of a warrant establishes a contract between you and the issuer, if the issuer defaults on its obligations then it is up to you to seek redress. It is important to note that the ASX, whilst being the platform for warrant trading, does not act as a guarantor for the issuer, just as it does not act as guarantor for any of the vehicles listed on the stock exchange.

As I mentioned earlier, one of my initial concerns about warrants was the lack of liquidity in the market. This problem has to a degree been alleviated by investor familiarity with warrants and a buoyant market. However, this is no guarantee that you will get what you deem to be a fair price in a thin market. The issuer is required to stand in the market. However, in the absence of anybody else they will stand in the market at a price that is favourable to them.

Normal market risks apply in warrant trading just as they do in ETOs. Warrants are just another financial tool and they respond to the vagaries of the market as does every other listed security. They are not a magic bullet, they will not guarantee you a profit despite what your broker has told you. Make an imprudent trading decision with warrants and you will lose money just as you would trading options or shares. The age-old rule of buyer beware applies.

LOW EXERCISE PRICE OPTIONS

The Low Exercise Price Option (LEPO) is a deep in-the-money European-style call option. It has an exercise price of between 1¢ and 10¢. Because it is so deep in-the-money it has a delta of approximately one. Hence they are a good proxy for share ownership.

When buying a LEPO, a trader puts up what is known as risk margin. This is generally 5 per cent of the purchase price of 1000 shares. If, for example, you were buying a LEPO in AMC and its market price was $9 then the LEPO would cost, 5% of 1000 x $9.00 = $450.

Despite the fanfare that accompanied them, LEPOs have not set the world on fire. Their liquidity remains poor and as such their uses are limited.

DOING THE BUSINESS

Chapter Nine

- ☑ **OCH Client Agreement Form**
- ☑ **Contract Notes**
- ☑ **Option Market Participants**

Let's assume that we have designed our strategy carefully, analysed the potential risks and defined our profit potential.

How do we actually enter the market and execute our trade?

OCH CLIENT AGREEMENT FORM

Firstly, before dealing in the options market, potential clients must sign an OCH Client Agreement Form, an example is given in Appendix A. This document basically stipulates that a client is aware of the mechanics of the options market, understands its risks and accepts being bound by its requirements. This form is a requirement of the OCH, not individual brokers; if this form is not lodged with the OCH, you cannot deal.

In addition to this, the options market has slightly different settlement requirements to those associated with dealing in equities. Settlement on options is required within 24 hours; in fact, most brokers will insist on a cash balance being established in your account before agreeing to enter the market on your behalf.

Having fulfilled these requirements, an order can now be placed with your broker. In placing your order, you must make several things clear:

(a) Whether the transaction is a buy or a sell

(b) The particular option to be bought or sold

(c) Whether the transaction is an opening or closing trade

(d) Whether the transaction is part of a strategy such as a spread

(e) The desired price.

It is worthwhile for a trader to write an order out in long hand such as:

Buy 10 BHP July 2000 calls at 65¢ to open

Taking such an approach will help avoid errors which are difficult to reverse and may be costly. A word of caution: if your broker cannot understand your order, offer possible refinements, or if he says it cannot be done without explaining why, find a broker who can. An inexperienced broker who is hesitant may be tempted to experiment and gain experience by using your money. Such a situation is totally unacceptable and such a broker will eventually cost you money, either by failing to understand your instructions or by giving advice that is inappropriate.

CONTRACT NOTE

If a trade is successfully executed, then the OCH will generate what is known as a contract note, see Fig. 9.1. The contract note is very important and must be checked carefully for any errors. Your broker will receive a copy of your contract note the following day and, as a matter of routine, all trades should be confirmed.

Reading from left to right, the contract note contains the following information:

1. The ASX code for the option traded — each option has an abbreviated code.

2. The month and year that the options will expire.

3. The exercise price of the option.

4. The number of shares per contract. As stated earlier, this is usually set at 1000 shares per contract but this will vary if the underlying stock has a bonus issue during the life of the option.

Fig 9.1 Example of Contract Note

OPTION SERIES					TRADED PREMIUM	REF. NO.	LOTS TRADED	B/S	T/T	CONTRACT PREMIUM VALUE	FEES	COMMISSION		STAMP DUTY
ASX Code	Month/ year	Exercise price	Shares per lot	Type								RATE	AMOUNT	
1	2	3	4	5	6	7	8	9	10	11	12	13	14	15

5.   Whether the option is a put or a call.

6.   The price at which the option was traded.

7.   Reference number.

8.   The number of contracts bought or sold.

9.   Whether the option was bought or sold. This section should be checked carefully. If an error has been made in registering a trade it should be reversed as soon as possible.

10. If the transaction was opening or closing.

11. The total contract premium, i.e. 6 x 7.

12. The Option Clearing House fees are set in the following manner:

Number of Lots	Fee per Contract
1-9	$1.50
10-19	$1.40
20-49	$1.30
40-99	$1.20
100 and over	$1.10

Any transaction that is opened and closed within five working days is known as a jobber trade and no registration fee is charged.

13. Commission rate (as a percentage) and;

14. The total amount.

15. Stamp duty is no longer charged on options trades.

Let's assume that we have successfully executed the first part of our order and that the resultant contract note accurately reflects this. The next step is simply to watch how the strategy unfolds. Remember that prior to placing the order all contingencies had been explored. Therefore, if the strategy goes astray, there is no excuse for panicking. This next phase is up to you, a good broker will literally hold your hand during your first trade. However, don't expect him/her to do all the work for you. Specialist option dealers have many clients some who are exceedingly active and who may generate a great deal of business. So don't be surprised if your broker is not on the phone to you constantly — it's your strategy so it requires your input.

If a strategy goes well and is showing a good profit, there will come a time to close the strategy out. To close out a strategy requires a set of instructions that are the opposite to the initial opening instructions.

In our first example, our first instruction was as follows:

> Buy 10 BHP July 2000 calls at 65¢ to open

To close out this play, we would issue the following instruction:

> Sell 10 BHP July 2000 calls at 95¢ to close

Once again, to avoid confusion, you should write out your instructions to make sure they are accurate. Having done this, you will receive an additional contract note detailing this trade. Accompanying this will be a liquidation notice stating that the position has been terminated and any profit generated by the trade. If your strategy has involved margins and deposits, you will also receive a statement detailing what margins were called and the interest accrued.

OPTION MARKET PARTICIPANTS

It should be obvious to the reader that the options market does not function like the sharemarket, there are certain structural differences that traders must be aware of. These structural differences are merely a reflection of the different characteristics of options versus shares.

The most obvious difference between shares and options is that options are still traded on an open outcry system on a trading floor in Sydney, whereas shares are traded electronically. In trading options you will come across a variety of market participants who you have probably not heard of before.

Your first experience of these new participants will be courtesy of the Options Clearing House Pty Ltd. You will first notice the OCH when you sign a client agreement form which has been generated by them. The OCH is a subsidiary of the ASX and its prime function is to act as a clearing house for all trades that pass through the options market, thereby guaranteeing the performance of all contracts that pass through the options market. This function is extremely important since for effective operating the options market relies upon the inherent belief that all contractual obligations will be met.

For example, if your broker were to go head over heels the OCH would guarantee that any obligations that had been incurred by the broker would be honoured.

As a consequence of its role as a clearing house the OCH acts as a regulatory body that oversees the fair and efficient functioning of the options market. The OCH doesn't guarantee you will make money but it does ensure that your efforts are not undermined by a loosely run market.

When you buy and sell shares via SEATS you are generally dealing with another investor who has a contrary view to you. If you want to sell BHP a buyer can be found. Liquidity is not a major problem in the equities market, unless you are trading the so-called penny dreadfuls. This is not the situation with the options market. As has been said many times in this book options are a wasting asset, as the time to expiry nears their value declines. It is therefore possible that liquidity is a problem in options that are close to expiry or that are far out-of-the-money.

If options were traded like shares it would be possible that you could not get your orders filled in situations of low liquidity. To overcome this problem the options market has what are called Registered Traders (RTs). It is the role of the RT to make a market in certain option classes. Each RT is assigned a stock such as BHP and is obliged to make a two-sided market in all the option series in BHP. By a two-sided market I mean he must provide a bid and offer and deal in a minimum parcel of contracts.

However, RTs are not a public service function, they are either employees of broking firms or are individuals working their own account. Their role is therefore to make a dollar for themselves. This puts them in direct conflict with traders attempting to deal in options. As a new participant in the options market you must be aware of the role of RTs since often you will be dealing with them and not someone who has a contrary view to you on a given stock.

There are a few rules to observe when dealing with RTs. Firstly, as I said earlier, they are not a public service function. They are out to make a profit, therefore, they are a competitor of yours. Secondly, be very careful in your instruction to your broker about the prices you are willing to deal at. Do not be convinced by your broker to automatically pay what is termed the market price. The reason for this is simple. Between you asking what the market is and then deciding to hit the bid or offer the prices can change dramatically.

For example, let me repeat a conversation I had many times with my operators. The conversation would go something like this.

Me:	What's the market in ABC?
Operator:	25 bid ... 30 offer.
Me:	Buy 20 at market.
Operator:	20 bought at 40.
Me:	What the !!!! do you mean 40, the offer was 30.
Operator:	It was an RT.
Me:	Enough said.

If you can avoid it do not place an order such as buy 10 BHP July 2000 calls at market. Let your broker's floor trader define what the market is and what they think of the prices on offer. Good floor operators are worth their weight in gold.

Thirdly, do not chase the price of an option. It is possible for RTs to continually move the price of the option away from you without any movement in the underlying stock. On many occasions this reached the absurd stage of the value of puts I was trying to buy going up whilst the underlying stock was going up.

To circumvent these problems there are a few easy rules to observe. Do not deal in illiquid stocks. It is much easier to get set in highly liquid stocks for two reasons. There is competition between RTs in these stocks and it is highly likely that you will be dealing with another trader with a competing view. Thus it is much easier to not only get set in a given position but to also get out of that position. Finally do not, if you can avoid it, trade on a Friday afternoon. The liquidity in the market dries up dramatically in the afternoon. The great financial market tradition of the long lunch extends to the options market.

A FINAL WORD

Options are not the Holy Grail of trading, the harsh reality is that if you lose money trading shares then you will probably lose money trading options. Options are not a substitute for not knowing what you are doing. Make a poor trading decision and the game is over, in fact the end of the game will come far quicker and more spectacularly trading options.

It should be remembered that some option trading strategies offer you unlimited risk. If you get it wrong then it is possible that you will lose everything. I am not talking about losing your entire investment. I am talking about losing your house, car and everything you have in the bank. I am not trying to discourage you from trading options but I am trying to reinforce the need for a trading plan. Merely taking your broker's word for what to do is a ticket to the poor house. After all, if they knew what they were doing do you think they would be talking to you?

Reading this book is only the first step in your education as a trader; understanding how something works is far different from making it work.

Good Luck!

APPENDIX A

THE AUSTRALIAN OPTIONS MARKET — CLIENT AGREEMENT

I/We..

(full names)

of...

(address)

Account No...

hereby declare that:

1. I/We have received and read a copy of the Explanatory Booklet issued by The Australian Stock Exchange (Sydney) Limited in respect of The Australian Options Market and dealings in Exchange Traded Options.

2. I/We agree to be bound by the Articles, Rules, By-laws and Regulations of The Australian Stock Exchange (Sydney) Limited applicable to the trading of option contracts and the Regulations of Options Clearing House Pty Ltd.

3. I/We agree not to violate, either alone or in concert with others, the position or exercise limits referred to in the Explanatory Booklet.

4. I/We agree to observe the margin requirements as established pursuant to the Regulations of Options Clearing House Pty Ltd.

5.   I/We acknowledge a Clearing Members obligation to close out any contract or contracts in respect of which I/We fail to deposit the required margin, or make the required payments, within 24 hours, in the case of cash covered written positions, or within 48 hours in any other case, of the Broker making the required payments or depositing the required margin with OCH Pty Ltd, or as required by the Regulations of the Australian Options Market.

6.   I/We agree to maintain with a Clearing Member a deposit or bank guarantee for such sum as shall from time to time be determined by the Board of The Australian Stock Exchange (Sydney) Limited, with respect to my/our dealings in Exchange Traded Options.

Signed at Sydney this   day of   19

Clearing Members Stamp   ....

....

....

(See Extracts from Options Trading Regulations — Appendix B)

APPENDIX B

EXTRACTS FROM AUSTRALIAN STOCK EXCHANGE (SYDNEY) LIMITED OPTIONS TRADING REGULATIONS

(a) Approval of Client's Account

No Member Organisation of Clearing Member shall accept an order from a client to take or write an Option unless:

(i) The client's account has been approved for Options transactions in accordance with the provisions of this Regulation and,

(ii) The client has on deposit with the Member Organisation or Clearing Member such sum as may be determined by the Board from time to time or has lodged with the Member Organisation or Clearing Member and has not withdrawn a bank guarantee for not less than that amount.

(c) Agreements to be Obtained

Within 15 days after a client's account has been approved for Options transactions, a Member Organisation or Clearing Member shall obtain from the client a written agreement in such form as may be determined from time to time by the Board that:

(i) The client is aware of and agrees to be bound by the Articles, Rules, By-laws and Regulations of the Exchange applicable to the trading of option contracts and the Regulations of Options Clearing House and,

(ii) The client agrees not to violate, either alone or in concert with others, the position limits established pursuant to these Regulations or the exercise limits established pursuant to these Regulations.

(d)   **Explanatory Booklet to be Furnished**

At or prior to the time a client's account is approved for Options transactions, a Member Organisation or Clearing Member shall furnish the client with a current Explanatory Booklet. Thereafter, each new or revised current Explanatory Booklet shall be distributed to every client having an account approved for Options trading, or, in the alternative, shall be distributed not later than the time a confirmation of a transaction is delivered to each client who enters into an Option.

(h) **If**

(i)   Within 24 hours, in the case of a cash covered writer, or within 48 hours in any other case, of a Member Organisation or Clearing Member making a payment to OCH Pty Ltd, a client fails to make payment of sums payable to the Member Organisation or Clearing Member (whether by way of premiums, deposits, margins, differences, security or otherwise), or to effect delivery or payment following allocation of an Exercise Notice.

(ii)   A Client withdraws a deposit or bank guarantee lodged in accordance with Regulation 015 (a)(ii), or

(iii)   A client suspends payment,

then the Member Organisation or Clearing Member shall forthwith, without the necessity of giving prior notice to the client, liquidate all or any particular Options in that Client's overdue and unsettled positions either, at the option of the Member Organisation or Clearing Member, by buying in or selling out against the same.

APPENDIX C

BROKERAGE RATES PER SLIDING SCALE

TO	$5,000	2.50%
ON NEXT	$10,000	2.00%
ON NEXT	$35,000	1.50%
ON NEXT	$100,000	1.00%
ON NEXT	$250,000	0.75%
OVER	$500,000	0.50%

CONTRACT AMOUNT	BROKERAGE	RATE
$15,000	$325	2.11%
$20,000	$400	2.00%
$25,000	$475	1.90%
$30,000	$550	1.83%
$40,000	$700	1.76%
$50,000	$850	1.70%
$60,000	$950	1.68%
$70,000	$1,050	1.50%
$80,000	$1,150	1.44%
$90,000	$1,250	1.39%
$100,000	$1,350	1.35%
$150,000	$1,850	1.23%

CONTRACT AMOUNT	BROKERAGE	RATE
$200,000	$2,225	1.11%
$250,000	$2,600	1.04%
$300,000	$2,975	0.99%
$350,000	$3,350	0.96%
$400,000	$3,725	0.93%
$450,000	$4,100	0.91%
$500,000	$4,475	0.90%
$550,000	$4,725	0.86%
$600,000	$4,975	0.83%
$650,000	$5,225	0.80%
$700,000	$5,475	0.78%
$750,000	$5,725	0.76%
$800,000	$5,975	0.75%
$850,000	$6,225	0.73%
$900,000	$6,475	0.72%
$950,000	$6,725	0.71%
$1,000,000	$6,975	0.70%
$1,500,000	$9,475	0.63%
$2,000,000	$11,975	0.60%
$2,500,000	$14,475	0.58%

GLOSSARY

American option

An American style option allows the holder of the contract to exercise at any time during the life of the contract up to and including the day of expiry. All exchange traded options traded in Australia are American in style.

Arbitrage

Arbitrage is used by professional investors to take advantage of price anomalies that may occur between two markets. For example if an arbitrageur decides that a given option is overpriced relative to its underlying stock they may choose to buy the stock and sell the option.

At the money

An option is said to be at the money when its exercise price is equal to the current market price of the underlying security. For example a BHP 1850 call would be at the money when BHP was trading at $18.50. Similarly a BHP 1850 put would be at the money also.

Average down

In my opinion, to buy more of a security the price of which has declined is a recipe for disaster. This is akin to hanging onto the deck of the Titanic as it went down.

Barrier Warrants

A barrier warrant is a standard warrant that has an enforced upper or lower limit. If the warrant closes beyond the barrier for a predetermined number of trading days, it expires, irrespective of how much time is left till the stated expiry date.

Basket warrant

A warrant that has been issued over a basket of shares. For example an institution may issue a warrant over the four major banks or a select group of resource stocks.

Bear/bearish

A bear is someone with a negative expectation of the market or a given stock. If I bought ANZ puts I would be bearish ANZ since I would be expecting a fall in price.

Bear spread

Creating a spread involves the simultaneous writing of an option with a lower strike price whilst purchasing an option with a higher strike price, usually with the same expiry date. For example if I were to sell the BHP 1850 call and buy the 1900 call I would have created a call bear spread. Such a strategy would have only a limited profit potential.

Beta

The degree to which a stock moves relative to the market. For example if a stock has a beta of 1.50 then for a given move in the market this stock will move an additional 50%.

Board broker

The board broker is an employee of the OCH who executes public limit orders on behalf of various clearing members.

Break even point

The price at which a trade neither makes nor loses money.

Bull/bullish

Someone who is a bull has an expectation that the market will rise.

Bull spread

Constructing a bull spread involves buying a lower strike price option at the same time selling an option with a higher strike price.

Buy and write

A buy and write which is sometimes referred to as a scrip covered write involves simultaneously purchasing shares and then selling a number of calls that are equivalent to the number of shares that have been purchased. Buy and writes enable traders to potentially increase the rate of return they achieve by holding shares at the same time providing a limited degree of downside protection.

Calendar spread

Constructing a calendar spread involves writing a near-month option and buying a far-month option at the same strike price.

Call option

A call option gives the holder the right but not the obligation to buy a fixed number of shares at a given price at any date up to a fixed expiry date.

Called away

Being called away refers to the process when the writer of a call option is required to sell the underlying security to a call option buyer as part of fulfilling their obligations. Being called away is something the naked option writer fears.

Carrying cost

The interest expense involved in purchasing an options position.

Cash covered option

A written option that has had cash lodged as security with the OCH. Also referred to as a naked options position since there is no underlying security to support the position in the event of the stock being called away.

Class deposit

The initial value of cash or collateral that is required to be paid by a naked option writer to the OCH. The level of deposit required is set by the OCH and varies from share to share.

Clearing member

A member organisation of the ASX which has been admitted as a clearing member of the OCH. A clearing member is generally the broker you deal through, and is entitled to trade on the floor of the OCH on behalf of clients.

Closing call prices

Also known as CCPs, these are the daily closing buy and sell prices for puts and calls. CCPs are used to establish daily margin requirements.

Closing purchase

Any trade that liquidates a trader's written option position. For example if I had written CBA 1000 calls then the transaction that buys these calls back is referred to as a closing purchase.

Closing sale

Any trade that liquidates a trader's bought position. For example if I had BHP 1800 puts and I sold them then this would be a closing sale.

Collar

A strategy that requires a trader to simultaneously write a put (call) and buy a call (put) in the same security but with different exercise prices. The aim of the strategy is to establish an upper and lower limit within which the strategy will generate a profit. You effectively put a collar around the stock.

Collateral cover

A value the OCH assigns to any security be it shares, bank guarantees or any other instrument that is lodged with the OCH as security for margins and deposits.

Combination

Any trade that involves simultaneous buying and selling of puts and calls with different exercise prices and/or expiry dates.

Contingent order

An order where one leg of a transaction is dependent upon another. For example if I were establishing a bull spread I might make the short leg of the trade contingent upon getting the long leg in place.

Cum

Latin word meaning with. Cum bonus, cum rights, cum dividend are all conditions that attach to the underlying security.

Currency Warrants

Currency warrants entitle the holder of the warrant to exchange an amount of a foreign currency for an equivalent amount in Australian dollars.

Delivery

The act of fulfilling your obligations under the terms of the option contract that you have incurred as the writer of that option. For example if I have written BHP 1900 calls and I am required to deliver then I must sell to the option buyer BHP at $19.

Delta

The degree to which an option price will move given a movement in the underlying security. An option with a delta of 0.5 will move half a cent for every full cent movement in the underlying stock. Deeply out-of-the-money calls have a delta approximating zero, at the money calls 0.5 and deeply in-the-money calls have a delta approximating 1.

Delta spread

A spread that is established as neutral position using the deltas of the options involved.

Diagonal spread

A strategy that requires a trader to write one option and take another option. Each option will have the same underlying security but will have different exercise prices and expiry dates.

Discount

An option is said to be trading at a discount when it is trading for less than its intrinsic value.

Downside protection

Insurance against any downward move in the underlying stock. Buying puts against physical stock or buying and writing confer downside protection.

Early exercise

Not something a naked option writer looks forward to. Early exercise refers to any option that is exercised prior to the expiry date.

Endowment warrant

A warrant where the outstanding balance is paid for by the accumulation of dividends from the underlying share.

ETO

Exchange traded option.

European option

An option contract that only allows exercise on the date of expiry.

Exercise

To invoke the right that is attached to an option contract. For example if I own a call option I have the right to buy the underlying stock at a given price. If I choose to take up the underlying stock I have exercised my right under the terms of the contract.

Exercise limit

The number of options that may be exercised over a given security in any given period. Exercise limits are seen in action during a takeover. They are designed to prevent traders from gaining a dominant position in the shares of a given company via the options market.

Exercise notice

Not something the naked option writer wants to see. An exercise notice is issued by the OCH and instructs an option writer to, in the case of a call writer, deliver stock at the exercise price specified; or for a put writer to take delivery of the stock at the specified exercise price.

Exercise price

The strike price of an option. It is the price at which an option may be exercised.

Expiration

The date at which all unexercised options lapse.

Expiration cycle

The time intervals between the option series. Whilst many options have what are termed spot months, the typical option has a three-month cycle based upon one of the following cycles:

January/April/July/October
February/March/August/November
March/June/September/December.

Expiry month

The month in which an option expires.

Fair value

The theoretical price of an option as defined according to a mathematical pricing model. Because each model has a variety of variables differing fair values will be obtained by a range of models. A cynic would argue that fair value can be defined as any price that you, the trader, doesn't pay.

Far month

The option series with the longest time to expiry.

Good until cancelled

A fairly rare order in options markets. If I were to give my broker an order to buy BHP July 1900 calls at 95¢ and add the proviso that the order was good till cancelled my broker would reinstate the order at the beginning of each day. Options orders are generally day-only due to the inherent volatility of the market.

Hedge

Any strategy or trade that reduces a trader's risk to adverse price movements.

Historical volatility

A measure of how much a share price has moved over a given period of time.

Holder

Any purchaser of an options contract.

Implied volatility

The potential for the price of the underlying security to move based upon the current option premium. When an option price is calculated using a mathematical model a number of variables are input into the equation. These variables include time to expiry, the price of the underlying share, dividends and the current level of interest rates and volatility. If the current option price and the theoretical price are in agreement then it can be assumed that the volatility used in the equation is correct. By manipulating the equation it is possible to obtain a figure for the volatility of the underlying share. The volatility is said to be implied since it was derived from the current price of the option.

In the money

When the exercise price of a call (put) is below (above) the current market value of the underlying security. For example if BHP were trading at $19.00 then an 1850 call would be said to be in the money. Whereas a put would be in the money only if its strike price were above $19.00, e.g.1950.

Index option

An option over a share index.

Index warrant

A warrant over a particular share index.

Initial deposit

Cash that has been lodged with a clearing member (your broker) by any trader who has written a naked option or cash covered position.

Intrinsic value

In-the-money options are said to possess intrinsic value. It is the difference between the exercise price of the option and the price of the underlying security. For example if NAB were at $19.10 then an NAB 1850 call which was trading at 70¢ would be said to have an intrinsic value of 60¢ (1910 - 1850 = 60) and a time value of 10¢ (70 - 60 = 10¢).

Legging it in

A mechanism whereby option trades involving many variables such as complex spreads are assembled one leg at a time instead of simultaneously. It is possible that in doing so you expose yourself to the risk that the market may move suddenly between the establishment of each leg thereby destroying the underlying reason for the strategy. In terms of risk it is analogous to straddling an electric fence as opposed to hurdling it.

LEPO

Low exercise price option.

Liquidity

The level of trade in a given option. Many option stocks are notoriously illiquid making them extremely difficult to trade. As a rule of thumb traders should not stray too far away from BHP, NAB, ANZ, CBA, WBC, NCP, WMC, RIO.

Long position

Any trader who has bought options is said to be long either the market or the underlying security.

Long term options

Options with expiry dates of two and three years.

Margin

When you write an options position there are certain market conditions that will impact adversely upon your position. If you are a call writer a lift in the market will damage your position. Likewise if you are put writer a fall in the market will degrade your equity. To compensate for these fluctuations the OCH calculates a daily margin based upon the movement of your option. The purpose of a margin is to protect your clearing member and by extension the OCH against any potential losses that may be incurred by a movement against your position.

Mark to the market

The process by which margins are calculated using the closing call prices.

Market maker

See *registered trader.*

Market order

An instruction to your broker to buy or sell at the prevailing market price. Something to be wary of.

Naked option

A position where the writer of an option does not own the underlying security. By definition all written puts are naked.

Neutral

A situation where you expect the market to remain fairly constant. You are neither bullish nor bearish. An example of a neutral strategy would be a written straddle.

Neutral price hedge

A strategy constructed so that any movement in the value of the long position is compensated for by an equal upward movement in the value of the short position. For example if I owned shares against which I had bought the appropriate number of puts. Any downward move in the value of the shares is compensated for by a move up in the value of the puts.

Offsets

A reduction in margin payments that are available to option traders as a result of holding positions of the same class.

Open interest

A measure of liquidity. It defines the number of outstanding contracts in a given option series.

Opening purchase

Any transaction in which a trader becomes the buyer or taker of an option.

Opening sale

Any transaction in which the trader becomes the writer of an option.

Options Clearing House (OCH)

The OCH is the overseer of the options market. It acts as the registrar of the market in that it guarantees the performance of all contracts, monitors and imposes margins, and reviews the financial situation of member firms. The OCH plays a prime role in generating confidence in the efficacy and professionalism of the market.

Out of the money

A call option with a strike price greater than the price of the underlying security or a put option with a strike price lower than the price of the underlying security. It is therefore obvious that an out-of-the-money option has no intrinsic value, its premium is therefore a reflection of purely time value.

Overvalued

A catch-all term used to describe anything that is trading at a higher than expected value.

Parity

Parity is achieved when an option is trading at intrinsic value only.

Pay-off diagrams

The funny little charts that litter this book. Typically they are used to give a visual interpretation of the range of outcomes for various strategies.

Position limit

The maximum number of options contracts that may be held by one trader.

Premium

Another word for the price of an option.

Price spread

Any option strategy that uses options of the same expiry dates but with different exercise prices.

Profit range

The prime consideration for any trader. It is the range of prices within which an options strategy will make a profit.

Put option

An options contract that gives the buyer the right but not the obligation to sell a fixed number of shares at a given price on or before an expiry date.

Random selection

The method by which the OCH assigns exercise notices.

Ratio strategy

Any strategy that involves unequal numbers of options.

Registered Traders (RTs)

I have heard many definitions of RTs over the years, most are unprintable. Because options are a wasting asset there is the possibility that as expiry nears liquidity in a given options series will dry up. To counter this problem the OCH appoints RTs who are obliged to make a market in their appointed stock. RTs have to provide a bid and offer for a minimum number of contracts thereby insuring liquidity. That's the theory.

Return if exercised

The amount of profit that a scrip covered writer may expect if the option they have written is exercised.

Return if unchanged

The profit that may be expected if the price of an underlying security does not alter before expiry.

Roll down

The closing out of all options positions in a given series and at the same time opening new positions in the same series but at a lower strike price.

Roll up

The closing out of all options positions in a given series and at the same time opening new positions in the same series but with a higher strike price.

Rolling

Closing of any option position in a given series and at the same time opening a new position in the same option series.

Scrip covered option

An option in which the writer owns the underlying security.

Series of options

Options with the same characteristics, i.e. strike price and expiry date.

Short selling

The strategy of selling an instrument that you do not already own in the belief that the price will fall and the security can be bought back at a lower price.

For example if I were to short sell BHP at $19.00 my belief would be that I could buy it back at below $19.00.

Spot options

Options which have a life span of one month from the time of listing.

Spread

Any strategy that involves the simultaneous buying and selling of options.

Spread orders

Requires that buy and sell orders be executed simultaneously. You know your broker has a good operator if he can pull this off without too much drama.

Straddle

A strategy that requires the simultaneous buying or selling of equal numbers of puts and calls with the same expiry date and strike price.

Strangle

A strategy that requires the buying or writing of two options, a put and a call. The strategy requires that the options used must be of the same expiry date but with different strike prices. The object of a strangle is to squeeze a stock between two strike prices.

Strike price

See *exercise price.*

Taker

Another word for the buyer of an option.

Theoretical value

See *fair value.*

Time value

The amount by which an option's value exceeds its intrinsic value.

Uncovered option

See *naked option.*

Undervalued

When an option is trading at a value lower than the theoretical price.

Volatility

The degree to which the price of an underlying security could reasonably be expected to move.

Warrant

An option that has been issued by a third party and is traded on the ASX.

Writer

The seller of an option.

INDEX

THE *ART* OF TRADING

TRADING SEMINARS

Seminars are conducted regularly throughout the year in all capital cities, and cover the following topics:

- ➤ The psychology of trading
- ➤ Trading method design
- ➤ How to be a more profitable trader
- ➤ The importance of the trend.

COUNSELLING AND COACHING FOR TRADERS

- ➤ Individual assistance for traders wishing to achieve their maximum potential.

TRADING SYSTEMS DESIGN

- ➤ Specialist trading systems available for both Supercharts and Metastock.

The Art of Trading P/L also presents two new video courses by Christopher Tate. These courses are specifically designed to guide you through uncertain times. In this new video series, this best-selling author and popular speaker will guide you through his pragmatic approach to demystifying the markets. You can also contact The Art of Trading for information about the author's trading newsletter, or visit the web site below.

For further information, contact:

The Art of Trading P/L
PO Box 1171
Caulfield North, VIC 3161

Email: **c_tate@malvern.starway.net.au**

Web site: **www.daytraderHQ.com.au**